DISASTER

CHALLENGES, RESPONSES AND MANAGEMENT

DISASTER

CHALLENGES, RESPONSES AND MANAGEMENT

By

Keshao Shankar Patil
&
Shankar Das

DPH

DISCOVERY PUBLISHING HOUSE PVT. LTD.
INDIA

Published by:
Namit Wasan
DISCOVERY PUBLISHING HOUSE PVT. LTD.
4383/4B, Ansari Road, Darya Ganj
New Delhi-110 002 (India)
Phone : +91-11-23279245; 23253475; 43596065
E-mail : discoverybooksindia@gmail.com
discoverypublishinghouse@gmail.com
namitwasan9@gmail.com
web : www.discoverypublishinggroup.com

***First Edition:* 2019**

ISBN: 978-93-86841-79-7

Disaster: ***Challenges, Responses and Management***

Printed at:
Infinity Imaging Systems
Delhi

Foreword

In the history of mankind the worst natural disasters have claimed innumerable lives and have caused millions of property damage. Since several years India has been affected by a number of worst natural disasters like floods, earthquakes, tsunamis, cyclones, landslides and severe weather conditions. Some of the devastating natural disasters such as Uttarakhand Floods in 2013, Tsunami in 2004, Gujarat Earthquake in 2001, Odisha Super Cyclone in 1999, Latur Earthquake in 1993 etc. have claimed many lives and have caused millions in property damage. The disasters lead to heavy losses of lives, mass casualties that can inundate existing health care services and resources and often thwart the delivery of medical and public health care.

The present book written by Prof. Keshao Shankar Patil and Prof. Shankar Das – two foremost experts in the field of disaster related research, training and interventions. This is the best book available to help students, teachers, practitioners of disaster related work to learn about theories and practices in disaster management. The authors of the book *Disaster: Challenges, Responses and Management* made a modest attempt and filled a major gap in the literature with a thorough introduction to the major conceptual underpinnings that are currently used to study the areas of disaster mitigation and management. This book examines a wide range of subjects relevant to studying disaster, mitigation, and disaster management in a clear and approachable manner.

The authors incorporate a broad scope of work from multidimensional perspectives while providing direction for future theory and practice pertaining to prevention, control and management of disasters. The issues discussed in the books are:

- An overview of concepts and practice in disaster mitigation and management
- Key concepts in disaster management
- Lessons from the field: Case studies in disaster management
- Role of higher educational institutes in disaster management
- Role of government and non-governmental organization
- Approaches, strategies and practices in disaster management

The book certainly would be very useful to the academicians, practitioners, students and scholars from various disciplines such as social scientists, public health and social work. It will also be useful to higher educational institutes to create awareness of disasters and disaster management among students, teachers and non-teaching staff. I am pleased for the efforts taken in writing and placing this valuable information to large audience. The repository of information in this important writing will go along way to serve as directions for planning and implementation of various programmes in the country.

Dr. Robin D. Tribhuwan
M.A., M.S.W., P.G.D.M., Ph.D.
Anthropologist and Development Expert

Preface

In this preface, we want to set the stage for reading this book for diverse audience. The subject of Disaster Management is widely debated and discussed world over. Natural disaster, occur in varied eco-climatic conditions. The Disaster Management experts and their team have to be prepared to prevent and control these disasters; experts have also classified disasters in two main categories such as natural and man-made disasters. Prevention and control of manmade disasters is also the responsibility of the concerned Government. The Developed countries have put in more efforts, time, energy and money studying the scientific causes of natural and manmade disasters. Hence awareness of disasters in developing countries is more as compared to the under developed countries.

The landslide in Malin village of Ambegaon tehsil in Pune district of Maharashtra state that nearly had swallowed the entire village could have been prevented, had the concerned Government agencies created awareness among the villagers, evacuated and resettled them in a suitable human safe habitats.

A developing country like India, where majority of the population resides in rural and tribal areas, there is a greater need for education among the people about various types of disasters, their causes, the preventive and restorative measures. People also need to know about the various agencies associated with prevention, control and management of different disasters. In India, large section of the population are unaware of their compensation rights, especially regarding loss of property, damages, loss of cattle and human lives.

As practitioners and researchers in a field of disaster management, we felt there is a need to inspire and motivate higher educational institutes of both science & social science faculties to create awareness of disasters, their prevention, control and management among the students, teachers as well as office staff. An attempt has been made to unveil the role of higher educational institutes in disaster management, including Government and Non-Government agency's role as well.

This book also has academic utility besides the practical one. The students, researchers and teachers of social sciences, public health and allied sciences will truly benefit from this book.

Keshao S. Patil
Shankar Das

Acknowledgement

It gives us great pleasure to place on record the valuable contributions made by many towards the successful completion of this book. We especially appreciate the time and efforts of the manuscript reviewers, who offered constructive criticism and supportive commentaries, as well as those academicians who provided us with constructive feedback that has been most useful in this book.

We thank Dr. Robin D. Tribhuwan, an eminent Anthropologist for writing the foreword and inspiring us to write this book.

Finally, we immensely thank our beloved family members for their continuous support and unconditional love - Dr. Panali Patil, Dr. Ashima Das, Mrinal, Priyal and Saptarishi, all deserves special mention and appreciations.

Keshao S. Patil
Shankar Das

Contents

1

Concepts and Practices in Disaster Mitigation and Management

Context

Since the time immemorial Disaster response was a natural survival mechanism in all human societies. Natural disasters are something that human race has had to deal with since the existence of humans. The natural calamities when they strike have the potential to wipe out considerable amounts of both human and wildlife populations. Actually, many opine that it is likely that a natural disaster will be the cause of the end of the world, when on earth that inevitably takes place. Yet to some extent they could be mitigated or avoided by preventive displacement of human population from areas where natural disaster are known to strike.

Since last four to five decades research dealt with systematic studies and survey on affected groups, impact and responses of affected, state and community preparations, recovery from natural and industrial disasters and other community level crises. Scientists have engaged in research that has increased our understanding of human cognition and responses to disaster, providing greater insight into how knowledge is organized, how experience shapes understanding and how people acquire expertise in managing future disasters. The field of research is to attempt to advance and communicate knowledge on mitigation techniques and procedures and disaster preparedness, response, and recovery. From this emerging body of research, case studies and anecdotal literatures the planners, policy makers, scientists and others may be able to synthesize a number of underlying principles of human learning on disasters.

At the beginning of the book the defining various concepts of the area may help in clarifying understanding about disaster, disaster mitigation and disaster management.

Definitions and Concepts

What is Disaster?

The word disaster is derived from Middle French désastre and that from Old Italian disastro, which in turn comes from the Ancient Greek pejorative prefix (dus-) "bad" and (aster), "star". The root of the word disaster ("bad star" in Greek) comes from an astrological sense of a calamity blamed on the position of planets (OED, 2018). The Oxford dictionary (2003) in simple terms defined a disaster is a sudden accident or a natural catastrophe that causes great damage or loss of life. Similarly Merriam-Webster Dictionary (2018) defined disaster as a sudden calamitous event bringing great damage, loss, or destruction. A disaster is an unanticipated occurrence disrupting and devastating the normal lives conditions of human existence and causing a degree of affliction that exceeds the capacity of adjustment of affected communities.

The International Federation of Red Cross and Red Crescent Societies (2017) and WHO (2002) defined "a disaster is a serious disruption, occurring over a relatively short time, of the functioning of a community or a society involving widespread human, material, economic or environmental loss and impacts, which exceeds the ability of the affected community or society to cope using its own resources". A disaster is a unexpected, calamitous incident that critically disturbs the normal functioning of a community or society and causes losses to human lives, material, and economic or environmental destructions that surpass the community's or society's capacity to cope using its own resources. Disaster often caused by nature, but may have human origins (IFRC, 2018). The United Nations defined disaster as "the occurrence of sudden or major misfortune which disrupts the basic fabric and normal functioning of the society or community" (In NIDM, 2014).

A disaster is a sudden, calamitous event that seriously disrupts the functioning of a community or society and causes human, material, and economic or environmental losses that exceed the community's or society's ability to cope using its own resources. Though often caused by nature, disasters can have human origins (UN-ISDR, 2018).

Ideally, a disaster may be defined as an event concentrated in time and space which threatens the society or a relatively self-sufficient division of the society with major unwanted consequences as a result of the collapse of precautions which hitherto been culturally accepted as adequate (Turner, 1977). People are considered to have been affected, if they require immediate assistance during a period of emergency to fulfil basic survival needs, such as food, water, shelter, sanitation and immediate medical assistance (Hays and Prepas, 2015).

Disasters are extreme events which cause great loss of life and property. They pose a serious threat to the normal life as well as the process of development and strike with sudden violence, tearing bodies, destroying lives and structures and throwing apart families. Thus, the impact of disasters on human life is multi-dimensional, affecting it in all aspects- domestic, social and economic etc.

Marathe (2006) marks that the words, "sudden" and "great". The word sudden indicates that such event is unexpected, unpredictable and the human is not prepared for it and great only means that the loss to life and property is beyond repairs or compensation and that the losses have a great bearing on the survivors, in fact, changing the courses of their lives. When the word disasters is used, it actually implies a wider encompassment in terms of coverage of geographical area, the intensity of catastrophe involving large number of lives and property and having greater effects on the society bringing about changes in economic, legal, cultural, political and administrative system.

In his paper captioned "Rethinking Disasters", Parasuraman (2013) stated that a clear definition of the term disaster is critical to shaping policy, practice and research. Hence the search for its right definition and the common minimum understanding assumes significance. Over the years, the term 'disaster' has come to have different meanings for different people.

Typically, it is used very loosely what Kreps (1984) calls a summative concept or what Quarantelli and Dynes (1970) call a "sponge word" that covers a range of meaning and situations. This conceptual haziness in understanding disaster is a hindrance in evolution of effective state policy, disaster preparedness, planning, mitigation and response and rehabilitation.

Anthropologists interpret disaster on the basis of people's perceptions and notions of why natural and man-made disasters are caused. Emphasis by Anthropological studies also is laid on emic approach (inside view). Some societies associate causes of great floods, cyclones, earthquakes, landslides, fire in the forest, lightning etc. to Karma (deeds) in the past and present life, wrath of Gods and Goddesses, breach of religious taboos, wrath of cosmic beings and spirits, sins in the past and present birth. These beliefs are prevalent in tribal and rural societies, including nomads.

The scientists however, interpret the causes of natural disaster on scientific lines. Before getting into the understanding the concepts of disaster and disaster management with reference to interventions and preventive practices, we may undertake the understandings of broad categories or types of disasters in subsequent discussions.

Disast… …itigation

…er mitigation means the strategies and mechanisms …lopted to lessen or limit the adverse impacts of that…nd related disasters. Often the adverse effects of ha…er are difficult to prevent completely, however their th… extremities can be considerably reduced by various …ve and preventive strategies and actions. Various …tion measures encompass hazard assessment, risk …ng, community education and preparedness, engineering …iques, hazard-resistant construction as well as improved …ronmental policies and public awareness. Disaster …igation is the course of actions that reduce or eliminate … impacts and risks of calamities through preventive and …roactive strategies adopted before a crisis or disaster take …lace. One of the best documented examples of investment in disaster mitigation is the Red River Floodway first used in 1969 which was artificially built partly in response to control the disastrous 1950 flood. Since its completion in 1968 the floodway has prevented over $40 Billion (CAD) in cumulative flood damage in Western Canada (GoM, 2017). The floodway is an exceptional engineering accomplishment both in terms of utility and effectiveness.

Disaster Management

Disaster management means systematic organization, planning, implementation of actionable strategies, responding to and recuperating from disasters. Disaster management can be defined as "the organization and management of resources and responsibilities for dealing with all humanitarian aspects of emergencies, in particular preparedness, response and recovery in order to lessen the impact of disasters" (IFRC, 2018). Disaster management may not completely avert or eliminate the threats; however it focuses on creating and implementing preparedness and other plans to decrease the impact of disasters and rehabilitate the affected. In the absence of prudent disaster management plan and preparedness could lead to profound damage to life, property and national revenue.

Sometimes emergency management is a interchangeably with the term disaster managemen used in the framework of natural and technological haza ly for health emergencies. Whereas there is a large sy overlap, a disaster can also be hazardous incidences tha not account for severe disruption of the functioning community or society.

The disaster management or risk reduction plann strategy does not only provide the agenda for the specifi sector plans, but may focus on the delivery of initiatives at a national and global level strategy. These programmes may aim to address recognized gaps in the way the crisis situation related information and knowledge across multi-sectoral stakeholders are handled with reference to supporting funding for community resilience interventions and other Disaster Management interventions. With the establishment of decentralized Disaster Management policies and programmes at a local and regional level with fundamental and adequate technical support, information management systems and innovative coordination of capacities at various levels may go long way in this direction. By using innovative methods and approaches of National governments and civil society organisations can respond in developing both internal and external trends and better enable the regional bodies to respond to the needs during crisis.

Chandra (2011: i) points out disaster management is the discipline of dealing with and avoiding risks. It is a discipline that involves preparing for disaster before it occurs, disaster response example emergency evacuation, quarantine, mass decontamination etc.; and supporting and rebuilding society after natural or man-made disasters have taken place.

Disaster management aims to reduce human suffering and economic losses caused by natural and technological disasters. We do this by Helping the World Bank provide more strategic and rapid response to disasters, and promoting the integration of disaster prevention and mitigation efforts into the range of development activities.

In general, any emergency management is a continuous process by which all individuals, groups, and communities manage hazards in an effort to avoid or ameliorate the impact of disasters resulting from hazards. Effective emergency management relies on through integration of emergency plans at all levels of government and non-government involvement.

Activities at each level, individual, family, group, community affects the other levels. It is common to place the responsibility for governmental emergency management to institutions to the Army, police, and other departments. Some of the key concepts in disaster management are: communication system, disaster informatics, preparedness planning, rehabilitation research, mitigation, improvement, measures, relief, and discovery planning and psychosocial support to the victims.

Classification of Disaster

CRED (2016) defines a disaster as "a situation or event that overwhelms local capacity, necessitating a request at the national or international level for external assistance; an unforeseen and often sudden event that causes great damage, destruction and human suffering". The following classification of natural disaster subgroups and their main types are given in the same reference and for a disaster to be entered into the database; at least one of the following criteria must be fulfilled:

- 10 or more people reported killed;
- 100 or more people reported affected;
- Declaration of a state of emergency;
- Call for international assistance.

Natural Disaster Subgroup Classification

Geophysical	Hydrological	Meteorological
Earthquake Mass Movement (dry) Volcanic activity	Flood Landslide Wave action	Strom Extreme Temperature Fog
Climatological	**Biological**	**Extra-terrestrial**
Drought Glacial lake outburst Wildfire	Animal accident Epidemic Insect infestation	Impact Space weather

Source: CRED; 2016

Types of Disasters

Studies by Talwar and Juneja (2009), Marathe P.P. (2006), Parsuraman and Krishnan (2013), Singh Sarthak (2010), Sharma Arjun (2012), Singh R.B (2006), Chandra P (2011), have revealed that there are two basic broad types or categories of disasters. These are natural and man-made disasters. This also being debated that all hazards causing into disasters are not natural but actually it is human induced. Disasters may be classified between natural and manmade disaster as follows:

A. Natural Disaster and their causes

Natural hazards such as earthquakes or floods arise from purely natural processes in the environment. Let us briefly look at some of the natural disasters and their causes as interpreted by scientists from an etic and scientific point of view. These natural disasters are as below:

(i) Earthquakes

The earth crust is layered and there are two rock layers. The bottom one is continuous and the other a fractured one. Both the layers are floating on the semi-plastised molten mass of the mantle. The entire crust is moving perpetually and the crust has tectonic plates under the continents and oceans. There are 14 major known plates and apart from these. There are scores of faults (Cracks) in the upper crust. The plates are also in individual motions which are either 'converging', 'diverging' or 'lateral'. These forces have effect in terms of shaking earth's crust and also many times the molten mass flows out of fractures. Such motion generates tremendous forces.

An earthquake is the trembling of the earth's surface, due to unexpected discharge of energy in the Earth's lithosphere that creates seismic waves. Earthquakes can take place in different magnitude ranging in those that are so feeble that cannot be felt to those so severe enough that can throw people around and obliterate whole cities. The seismic activity of an area can determine the incidence, type and size of earthquakes experienced over a period of time.

These forces are effects in terms of shaking the earth's crust and also many times the molten mass flows out of fractures. The shaking of earth is what we call earthquakes. Sometimes earthquakes occur due to movement of the plates. Colonel Marathe (2006:7) states that earthquakes happen at the rate of 800 to 1000 per year. The earth is continuously vibrating with suck quakes.

Felt Effects of Earthquakes are:

- Crumbling of building, bridges, huts and other structures.
- People get buried under debris.
- Trees are uprooted.
- Roads and land tear or crack apart. Cracks appear in dams and flooding takes place because dams burst.
- Landslides occur, burying structures around.
- In industries, factories and nuclear plants, if damage to furnace occurs, it may result into leakage of the chemicals and also nuclear radiations.

Earthquakes are thus considered as the most damaging of disasters because of suddenness of the occurrence, the degree of damage, lack of warning systems and unpredictability of the place and time. The village, district, state or country that becomes a victim of earthquakes suffers financial social, physical and environmental including human losses. Educating people about the scientific aspects of earthquakes and minimum preventive precautions that need to be taken is a significant factor.

(ii) Floods

During the rainy season water accumulation rates go up. Water flows down the mountain slopes and then into streams and 'nallahas' and finally into rivers. The rivers carry water and washed down mud along their course. When the banks are shallow, the additional water starts spreading across the banks, inundating areas around. There is an upper limit to the quantum of water that can get accommodated within the river banks, with respect to the rate of discharge, measured in 'cusecs'. Floods occur when this limit is crossed.

In India when the Himalayan rivers receive greater water in summer due to melting of the snow. When this rate of melting of the snow exceeds certain limits, floods are caused. Some of the felt effects of the floods are as below:

- Land communications get cut off, marooning people for days.
- Electricity supply gets affected; broken live wires create secondary disasters of electrocution.
- Loss of lives due to drowning of people, cattle and poultry is heavy.
- The spread of water submerges ground, adversely affecting crops.
- The overflow of rivers causes water pressure to build up against structures, causing destruction.

Since floods have a particular pattern, in spite of the varying degree, vulnerability of the areas is known. This helps the government, NGOs and international organisations to take timely precautionary measures.

(iii) Cyclones

Cyclones are a regular occurrence on the east coast of India and also in the North American continent. Cyclones have different names viz.

- Hurricanes
- Blizzards

The only cause of a cyclone is the climatic disturbances created due to temperature and pressure variations. A cyclone or a hurricane is said to be formed when minimum wind velocity of 119 km/hr. below this scale the high wind condition is only called a 'storm'.

Landslides are mostly caused as secondary effects due to earthquakes, tsunami, cyclones, floods or heavy pre-capitation (rains). They are also caused due to natural denudation and soil erosion, depletion of tree cover.

(iv) **La[nd]slides**

[D]evelopment of roads and highways including tunnels [w]eaken the hill structure. Such areas are prone to landslides. [Such ar]eas become vulnerable with other natural calamities [like ea]rthquakes, floods and heavy rains and chances of [lands]lides increase manifold.

Marathe, (2006) reports that in august 2005, after Konkan [bel]t of Maharashtra experienced multiple landslides, a survey [w]as done and it was noticed that many hills had developed [v]ertical cracks in Sahayadri region, on the western slopes. Thus, that region would be threatened with landslides.

Some of the major effects of landslides cut off road communications and people trapped in it suffocate and get injured due to falling debris. Rescue is difficult as landslides leave a loose mass of earth.

(v) ***Fires***

Fire is a phenomenon of combustion of material. Fires are the most common of the disasters and are indeed avoidable. Fire is caused mainly due to human interventions. Forest fires are caused by natural phenomenon. Main reasons for fires to start are- the accidental ignition due to system failures (like in industries) or human errors, carelessness in the kitchen while operating stove and gas, unattended flames of candles and oil lamps, use of crackers at wrong places and in wrong manner and collisions due to automobiles or air accidents etc. Many a time process failure also occurs. Unscrupulous electric connection cause sparking and results in initiation of fire. Marathe, (2006) points out that fire has three main effects viz:

- Rise in temperature that causes surrounding material to catch fire.
- Smoke causes poisoning.
- Suffocation and destruction of property.

(vi) ***Heat Waves***

A heat wave is a prolonged period of excessively hot weather which may be accompanied by high humidity. There is no universal definition of a heat wave; the term i lative to the usual weather in the area a relative to nal temperatures for the season.

Heat waves form when high pressure (from 100 25000 ft.) strengthens and remains over a region for sev days up to several weeks. This is common in summ Hypothermia, also known as heat stroke, becomes commo place during period of sustained high temperature and humidity. Sweating is absent from 84% to 100% of those affected. Older adults, children and overweight people are at high risk.

(vii) Epidemics

An epidemic occurs when new cases of a certain disease in a given human population and during a given period, substantially exceed what is expected based on recent experience. Epidemiologists often consider the term outbreak to be synonymous to epidemic, but the general public typically perceives outbreaks to be more local and less serious than epidemics.

An epidemic may be restricted to one location, however if it spreads to other countries and continents and affects a substantial number of people, it may be termed a pandemic. The declaration of an epidemic requires a good understanding of a base line rate of the incidence.

(viii) Volcanic Eruptions

A volcano is a vent in the earth through which hot gases and molten rocks rise to the surface. A cone shaped mountain of erupted material around such a vent is also called a volcano (Sharma, 2012). The name is taken from the Volcano, an island north of Sicily in the Mediterranean Sea. The island is given its name by the ancient Romans because it spewed smoke like vapour, and was thought to be the home of Vulcan, the God of fire. A volcano that is erupting or has erupted during historic times is called active. A volcano in which there is no evidence of any activity is considered to be extinct. There are about 2500 known active volcanoes in the world.

There are many different kinds of volcanic activities and eruptions: Phreatic eruptions, explosive eruption of high silica lava, effusive eruption of low silica lava, pyroclastic flows and carbon-di-oxide emissions. All these activities can pose hazard to humans. Earthquakes, hot springs, fumaroles, mud pots and geysers often accompany volcanic activity.

B. Man Made Disasters

Manmade disaster arises directly as a result of human activities. Man-made hazards such as accidents, war, pesticide toxicity, accidental release of chemicals or radiation from a nuclear plant that are largely preventable. Manmade disasters are of following types are caused due to accidents or non-compliance or failures of safety measures and can be quite complex and varying in degree and encompassment of areas:

Industrial and other Fires

- Chemical/gas leakages
- Structural damage and collapse
- Air/rail/road/maritime accidents
- Nuclear radiation and biological leakages
- War-conventional and non-conventional
- Environmental degrades causing losses
- Hybrid disaster like terrorism, which include bomb explosions, kidnapping, killings and hijacking.
- Cyber relating crimes

Given below are a few examples of such manmade disasters.

(i) Explosions

With the onset of terrorism, explosions have attracted great attention. Terrorist organisations use explosive to cause damage and destruction and rein havoc amongst the population. An explosive is a substance that burns vigorously when ignited; causing such rapid chemical changes that great amount of mechanical force is creating causing a bursting effect.

Explosives are generally categorised as high explosives, low explosives and miscellaneous Compositions like smoke and incendiary. Explosions cause loss of life and destruction of property. Explosives cause causalities manly due to blast waves. Blast waves shatter surfaces of object. The next effect is due to splinters that embed in bodies. Effect due to heat is the least because of the greater dissipation of heat energy. Explosions due to gas cylinders also fall in the same category. Secondary fire may start due to explosions. The 9/11 attacks on the World Trade Centre in the United States caused a double pronged damage- one due to the impact of planes on the structures and second, due to explosions of the fuels in the planes, causing greater damage to the already damaged and loosened structures.

(ii) Accidents

Accidents could be air, road, rail or marine accidents. Most accidents are caused due to human errors. However, some accidents do occur due to environment conditions like- bad roads, poor visibility and adverse ground and weather condition. In India, accidents rates are phenomenally very high.

(iii) Nuclear, Biological and Chemical (NBC) Disasters

As the mankind has progressed, the usage of such agents has increased tremendously. Apart from the usage during war, accidentals leakages have occurred in the past. When one thinks of a war, scenes of Hiroshima and Nagasaki flash in our minds. This problem is becoming worse, with terrorist organisations getting more modern in their attacks.

Effects of nuclear, biological and chemical disasters lead to life loss and destruction of property.

This further has an adverse impact on the economy of the country or state affected by nuclear, biological and chemical disasters. Besides the physical losses, people have negative psychological impact due to such disaster.

(iv) Nuclear Energy Related Issues

The main effects are caused by Alfa, Beta, Gamma radiation. Human body can accept certain dosage of radiation without any ill-effects. Beyond a particular stage, the effects are irreversible.

(v) Explosions of an Atomic Weapon

Atomic weapons, when exploded could have devastating effects due to great speed of atomic fission or fusion or a combination of the two with 'critical mass' of a kind that results into production and release of great amount of energy. The threat of usage of nuclear weapons has grown over the past few decades. Thus there is need to create awareness and preparedness for such eventuality.

(vi) Chemical Agents

Bhopal gas tragedy can be considered as the severest of all accidents caused due to chemicals. The cyanide content of the gas produced in the factory leaked in December 1984 causing thousands of deaths and many more to suffer permanent damages to eye sights and respiratory systems. Given below are certain chemical agents and their effects.

- VX nerve gas-Disrupts nervous system, causes convulsions, respiratory failures, paralyses and death
- Sarin- attacks nervous system and can cause death within minutes.
- Mustard gas- Causes skin and eye burns, blisters and lung diseases and often cancer.

Disaster and Disaster Management

The India disaster report II, edited by Parasuraman and Unnikrishnan, (2013) revealed that natural and social systems are interconnected and looking at them dichotomously leads to problems further, most disaster have a clear and direct nexus with poverty. It is the poor people who always bear the brunt of disasters- let it be a flood, a drought or an earthquake. For example, a decade long studies from 1992 to 2002 show that disasters on an average kill 555 people in a low human development index country. The same disaster kills 133 people in a middle human development index country (IFRC 2004)

India's booming cities with their poor services, inadequate local governance and stark inequalities are often spots of present and future disaster. Several social scientists, technicians and disaster management have come up with different concepts. Given below are a few concepts.

(i) Linking Rivers

One of the concepts floated by Thakkar (2013) had stated that the policy makers are toying with grand plan- link 37 rivers through 30 link projects. The idea is to solve the countries flood and drought problems.

(ii) Dipping water levels: Looming crisis

Shripad, (2013) has put forth the concept of lack of water which is a slow onset disaster. Rivers are drying up, ground water resources are getting used up and lakes and lagoons are polluted. Big dams with big claims often fail. Still there is no effort to catch rains where it falls. The advocates of this concept advocate water harvesting.

(iii) Drought: Threatening food security

Mahapatra Richard (2013) has pointed out that drought has a class bias. It hits small and marginal farmers who feed the nation - the hardest. So it is a double whammy, marginalising a set of poor people and threatening the countries food security. Careful interventions, however, bring about changes.

(iv) Psycho-social care and support in Disaster

The mental and emotional responses among affected members of a community may vary from each other after any disaster. In addition this also may generally undergo changes over a period of time depending upon the socio-economic condition and the coping capacity of that community. Hence,

live lost were, 2606 and 2,628,855 houses were damaged. CWC reports that in the year 2008, 19.21 million people were affected With floods, 17214 cattle lost their lives, human lives lost were 2143 and 9,14,251 houses were damaged.

(ii) Earthquakes

According to the National Disaster Management, Guidelines for Management of Earthquakes (NDMA) 2008, about 59% of India's land area is vulnerable to moderate or seismic hazards, that is prone to shaking of Medveder-Sponheuer-Karnik (MSK) intensity and above.

The period 1990 to 2006 experienced 6 major earthquakes that have resulted in over 23000 deaths and caused enormous damage to property assets and infrastructure.

Table 1.1 presents a list of major earthquakes in India and its neighbourhood.

Table 1.1

Major Earthquakes in India

S.N.	Date	Latitude N	Longitude E	Location	Deaths
1.	15 August, 1950	28.5	96.7	Arunachal Pradesh-China border	1500
2.	21 July, 1956	23.3	70.5	Anjar, Gujarat	Hundreds
3.	10 December, 1968	17.37	73.75	Koyana, Maharashtra	200
4.	21 August, 1988	26.77	86.63	Bihar-Nepal border	1003
5.	30 September, 1993	18.07	76.62	Latur-Osmanabad, Maharshtra	7928
6.	22 May, 1997	23.08	79.42	Jabalpur, Madhya Pradesh	38
7.	29 March, 1999	30.41	79.42	Chamoli, Uttaranchal	06
8.	26 January, 2001	23.06	69.8	Kutch-Bhuj, Gujarat	20000

Source: India Meteorological Department (accessed on 30 October, 2012)

(iii) Most Intense Cyclones

India experienced nearly 15 most intense cyclones from 2004 to 2007 destroying several buildings, crops, structures, cattle, human lives and houses. Table 1.2 provides glimpses of a few cyclones.

Table 1.2

Glimpses of most Intense Cyclones

S.N.	Name of Cyclone	Date	Damage
1.	Sever cyclonic storm over Arabian sea	5-10 May, 2004	9 people dead, 17 missing. Total loss worth Rs. 30 crore
2.	Cyclonic storm over Bay of Bengal	14-17 October, 2001	108 people dead, 21 missing. Damage to crops about 125,000 hectares; and 55,747 houses in Andhra Pradesh
3.	Severe cyclonic storm over Bay of Bengal	11-16 December, 2003	81 people dead, in Andhra Pradesh, 1637 buildings destroyed completely, damaged 61,898.5 hectares of agriculture land
4.	Cyclonic storm SIDR	11-16 November, 2007	One person dead. 46 villages affected in West Bengal. Crops were damaged in thousands of acres of land

Source: India Meteorological Department

(i) Droughts and Famines in India

According to Down to Earth may 2001, 155 droughts and famines took place in India from 5th century BC up to 20th century AD.

(ii) Major Terrorist Attacks in India

Sinha, (2006) an IPCS special report, 27 July 2006, New Delhi reports that there were 17 major terrorist attacks in India from 2000 to 2006. Given below are few of them.

1. 20th, March 2000

On the eve of US president Clinton's visit, militants massacred 35 Sikhs in the village of Chattisinghpara. No group claimed the responsibility for the attack.

2. 13th, December 2002

Militants attacked the Indian parliament in which 9 policemen and Parliament staffers were killed. All five terrorists were killed by the security forces and were identified as Pakistani nationals.

3. 5th, July 2005

Six heavily armed militants, who made an attempt to storm the high security Ram Temple, were killed before they could reach the shrine.

4. 29th, July 2005

At least 10 people were killed and more than 50 others injured in the explosion of Shramjeevi express in Uttar Pradesh. Two Bangladeshi nationals were arrested by policemen at New Delhi station.

5. 25th August 2005

Two powerful car bomb explosions took place in Mumbai, killing at least 46 persons and injuring over 160. The second blast took place 4 minutes later close to the gateway of India, near the Taj Mahal hotel.

6. 11th July, 2006

A series of Bomb blast took place in local trains in Mumbai killing 190 people and injuring 165.

(vi) Major Chemical accidents in India (2002 to 2006)

According to the National Disaster Management Authority 2007 New Delhi, nearly 25 major chemical accidents in India were reported from 2002 to 2006.

Account of the Problem

Disaster occurs at the interface of the society, technology and environment are fundamentally the outcomes of the intersection of these features.... In very graphic ways, disasters serve as indices of the success or failure of the society to adapt, for whatever reasons, to certain features of its natural and social constructed environment in a sustained fashion (Oliver-Smith 2006).

Disaster prevention requires a more nuanced understanding of the natural and social systems and the limits of technological interventions. It requires an understanding of the causes, consequences and the complex dynamics of disaster. It requires more rigorous research, balanced thinking and a certain degree of humility. Researchers have pointed out that a key factor that influences disaster patterns and people's vulnerability to them is development intervention.

Safety, dignity and rights of people affected by the disaster are the key concern. Majority of the people who become victims of disaster are poor as aptly pointed out by Parasuraman and Krishnan (2013). Millions of people lose their lives every year across the globe due to natural and man-made disasters. The developed countries are usually prepared and are aware of the natural disaster at least and take maximum preventive precautions to prevent the same. Things are different, in a developing country like India.

Are the developing countries prepared to face the effects of natural and manmade disasters? Can they afford to bear the financial, physical, social and environmental loss due to disaster? How effective and scientific is their disaster management plan. What is the roll of social scientist, public health professionals and social works experts in the disaster management? What effective interventions need to be developed for a given disaster?

These and several other research questions haunt the mind of a researcher. One area that needs serious attention with regards to disaster and its management is the need to create awareness in school, colleges and even amongst people in rural, tribal and urban areas. The National Disaster Management Team should devise prevention model so as to develop preventive precautions.

Keeping in view the above background, the present book aims to unveil the concepts of disasters, its management, awareness and warning strategies, research and interventions, More specifically the main objectives of book are as follows:

Post Disaster Phase: Re-workout risk assessment and relay mitigation plans, undertake fresh reconstruction and development activities at the earliest carry out accounting funds, strengthens warning systems, reassess training and education needs in consonance with the national policies, disburse financial aids for rehabilitation and reconstruction, revise development norms.

District Development Management Authority

Preparatory Phase: Workout mitigation plans at Tehsil and district levels, conduct detailed risk assessment in the district, co-ordinate with mitigation organizations, co-ordinate with the NGOs in the district, place resources, keep dynamic communications ready, update survey data, create self-help groups and team, conduct training at community level, create detailed warning systems down to the lowest level.

Execution Phase: Issue warning, activate organization, deploy mitigation units, order resource mobilization, execute evacuation plans including establishment of control centers and ground zero controls, assess damage and report, activate self-help groups and NGOs, establish relief camps and disburse relief material, disburse compensation, commence rehabilitation and reconstruction.

Post Disaster Phase: Strengthen the warning system and re-evaluate evacuation plans, re-assess risk factors in the district, revise developmental plans, revise resource placement and mitigation plans, create more awareness, training and create stronger self-help groups.

Once disaster strikes, the above existing administrative set-up is required to swing up in to relief operations, if the Administration fails, there is utter chaos leading to further loss of lives and property. State government's needs to make full use of the existing plans schemes that will help in overcoming the conditions created by the calamity. As a first responder in any disaster situation, however, each state needs to build a team, trained and skilled personnel, make provision for specialized equipment, efficient communication network, and relevant, intelligent and easily accessible database. There is also need to consider creation of planned scheme in each state basically to meet the minimum requirements for strengthening communication and emergency control rooms, thereby improving coordination and response to disasters.

The book provides key information regarding natural and man-made disasters, there mitigation and management. It covers a broad spectrum of topics from the elementary understanding for the general public, for the students of social sciences and more particularly to the helping professionals and allied discipline, to the more advanced conceptual understanding of prediction, prevention, warning, risk, relief, mitigation and management of hazards.

It also provides the role of workers, volunteers, experts and students in designing appropriate interventions for a particular disaster. It provides case studies of a few disasters including its management methodologies and techniques, of disaster preparedness and rehabilitation.

At the theoretical level the data presented in the book will certainly pave way for social scientists develop new theoretical insights. On the other hand, at the more practical level, the book will be of immense help to students of social sciences and more particularly the students of behavioral sciences and social work.

2

Important Aspects in Disaster Management

Introduction

The field of Disaster Management is so vast and difficult for a common man to understand. In this chapter, the author has made an attempt to simplify certain key concepts in disaster management, so that a common man and more precisely a student of social science is able to understand the same. This chapter presents in simplified fashion the key concepts in disaster management. Most literatures on disaster management classify two types of disasters namely natural and man-made.

Sharma (2012) defines a natural disaster to a consequence when a natural hazard affects humans and/or the built environment. The man-made disasters are the consequences of technological or human hazards. Example of these disasters includes stampedes, fires, transport accidents, industrial accidents, oil spills, chemical spills, nuclear explosions etc. Some authors further sub-classify the two main types. These are as below:

A. Geological Hazards

Geological Hazards are basically natural. The terms and definitions of the same are given below:

1. **Avalanche:** An Avalanche is a geophysical hazard involving a slide of large snow (or rock) mass down a

mountainside, caused when a buildup of snow is released down the slope, it is one of the major dangers faced in the mountains in winter.

2. **Lahar:** A Lahar is a type of natural disaster closely related to a volcanic eruption and involves a large amount of material, including mud, rock and ash sliding down the side of the volcano at a rapid pace. These flows can destroy entire towns in seconds and can kill thousands of people.
3. **Earthquakes:** An Earthquake is a phenomenon in that result from and is empowered by the sudden release of stored energy that radiates seismic waves.
4. **Super volcano:** A Super volcano is an eruption which is thousand times larger than normal eruption. The last eruption of this kind occurred over 75,000 years ago (Sharma Arjun 2012:6).

B. Water Related Hazards

Some of the water related Hazards are:

- Flood
- Limnic eruption
- Maelstrom
- Tsunami
- Mega Tsunami

1. **Flood:** Prolonged rainfall from a storm, including thunderstorm, rapid melting of large amounts of snow, or rivers which swell from excessive precipitation upstream and cause widespread damage areas downstream, or less frequently bursting of man-made dams or levees.
2. **Limbic Eruption:** This is a rare type of natural disaster in which CO_2 suddenly erupts from deep lake water, posing a threat of suffocating wildlife, livestock and human beings.
3. **Maelstrom:** This is a large tidal whirlpool; speed can reach between 20 km to 40 km per hour.

Man-Made Hazards

F. Sociological Hazards

Sharma (2012) classifies five subcategories sociological Hazards under man-made disasters. These are:

- Crime
- Arson
- Civil Disorder
- Terrorism
- War

1. **Crime:** Crime is to breach the rules or laws for which some government authority can ultimately prescribe a conviction. Crimes of certain kinds create man-made hazards. For example burning houses of an enemy party or village or clan as it were killing people by planting a bomb.
2. **Arson:** Arson is a criminal intent of setting a fire with intent to cause damage.
3. **Civil Disorder:** Riot is the best example of civil disorder that causes disturbance to the civil society.
4. **Terrorism:** Terrorism is a controversial term with very definitions. One such definition means of violent action targeting civilians exclusively. Another definition states, the use or threatened use of violence for the purpose of creating fear in order to achieve a political, religious or ideological goal.
5. **War:** War is a conflict between relatively large groups of people, which involve physical force inflicted by the use of weapons. Warfare has destroyed entire cultures, countries, economies, and inflicted great suffering on humanity.

G. Technological Hazards

Sharma (2012) has classified technological hazards into following categories, namely:

- Industrial hazards
- Structural collapse
- Power outrage
- Fire

1. **Industrial Hazards:** Industrial disasters occur in a commercial context, such as mining accidents, chemical or gas leakage in a factory etc. They often have an environmental impact. The Bhopal disaster is the world's worst industrial disaster to date.
2. **Structural Collapse:** Structural collapses are often caused by engineering failures.
3. **Power Outrage:** The Power outrage is an interruption of normal sources of electrical power.
4. **Fire:** Bush fires, forest fires and mine fires started by lightning and also by you negligence is yet another technological hazard.
5. **Transportation Hazards:** Traffic accidents are a major cause of death and injuries worldwide, but while there are definitely declining in many parts of the developed world, fatalities are still on the rise in many developing countries including India.

Key Aspects in Disaster Management

Disaster management is an enormous task. They are not confined to any location; neither do they appear as quickly as they appear. Therefore it is imperative that there is a proper management to optimize efficiency of planning and response.

Disaster management is a cyclically process; the end of one phase is the beginning of another, although one phase of the cycle does not necessarily have to be completed in order for the next to begin. Often several phases are taking place concurrently. Timely decision-making during each phase results in greater preparedness, better warnings, reduced vulnerability and/or prevention of future disasters. The complete disaster management cycles includes the shaping of public policies and plans that either addresses the causes of disasters or mitigates their efforts on people, property and infrastructure (Sharma, 2012).

The mitigation and preparedness phase occur as improvements and are made in anticipation of an event. By embracing development, a community's ability to mitigate against and prepared for disaster is improved. As the even unfolds, disaster managers become involved in the immediate response and long-term recovery.

Given below are the brief explanations of certain key aspects of disaster management:

1. **Mitigation:** Measures put in place to minimize the results from disaster. Some examples of this are: building courts and zoning, while a rebel itty analysis, public education and so on.
2. **Preparedness:** Planning how to respond to disaster or hazard as it were. Examples of this are preparedness plans, emergency exercises/training, warning systems.
3. **Response:** Initial actions taken as the event that takes place. It involves efforts to minimize the hazards created by disaster. Some of the examples of this are evacuation, search and rescue, and emergency relief.
4. **Recovery:** Returning the community to normal. Ideally, the affected area should be put in a condition equal to or better than it was before the disaster took place. Some of the examples of this are housing, grants, medical care, etc.

   Chandra (2011:1) while discussing the communication system in disaster management reveals the concept of Emergency Management Information System.
5. **Emergency Management Information System** (EMIS) is a computer database for disaster response that provides graphical real-time information to respondents. He further states that are four phases of an EMIS are:
   (i) ***EMIS for preparedness:*** This includes:

- Preparation of contingency plans for different types of emergencies;
- Creating checklists that can be easily reached by any related emergency management stakeholder;
- Resource management

(ii) ***EMIS For Risk Mitigation***

- Data mine possible risk areas and/or risk types. Often supported by a geographical information system (GIS)

(iii) ***EMIS for Response***

- Executing and tracking the contingency plan

(iv) ***EMIS for Recovery***

- Cost calculation of the emergency
- Various kinds of reports, supported by tables, graphs, etc.

6. **Logistics Support System**

Logistic support system (LSS) is a tool for the purpose of facilitating the communication among humanitarian agencies, non-governmental organizations, donors, media or countries and enhancing the coordination process and supply chain. Two modules of logistics support systems have been created, namely:

(i) A model that operates under Windows systems

(ii) the module that operates under Internet Explorer

7. **Amateur Radio Emergency Communications**

In times of crisis and natural disasters, amateur radio is often used as a means of emergency communication, when Wire line, cellphones and other conventional means of communications fail. Some of the examples of these are:

- Aircraft emergency frequency
- Distress signal
- Maritime
- Storm spotter

Rehabilitation

Depending on the degree of damage caused, loss of life and property, the next step is rehabilitation of the survivors. If the survivors are orphaned children, the rehabilitation strategies have to be worked out so as to send them to boarding schools, orphanages or rehabilitation centers. The question of their further education, service and survival need to be given serious thought to. Rehabilitation programs vary to one country to another, from one NGO to another. Rehab policies too vary.

3

Lessons from the Field

Case Studies in Disaster Management

Introduction

This chapter presents a several cases of disasters that occurred in India. The objective of this chapter is to throw light on the reason for the occurrence of a disaster, the various strategies implemented by the government, the response of NGOs, media, the survivors, relatives of the victims and citizens groups and also attempted to capture how political leaders handled and perceived the incidence. To begin with the case of a recent disaster of landslide that took place in Malin village of Ambegaon tahsil of Pune district in the state of Maharashtra, India.

Landside Swallows a Village in Pune District

A. The locale of the disaster

It is situated about 110 km away from Pune city. Malin village surrounded by hills on all the sides-had 500 registered voters and a population of 750 people, largely dominated of the scheduled tribe community. The residents belong to the Koli Mahadev tribe. On 31 July 2014, a landslide occurred in the village of Malin in the Ambegaon taluka of the Pune district in Maharashtra, India. The massive landslide, hit the village early in the morning while most people were asleep. It is reported that the cause is due to burst of heavy rainfall, and total death toll was about 151 people (Indian Express, 2014). In addition to the death toll, more than 160 people and probably up to 200 were reportedly to have been buried in the landslide in 44 different houses (Indian Express, 2014). Incessant rains after the landslide made the rescue operation difficult.

B. The reasons for the disaster

There were 45 houses in the hamlet, which were buried, when a part of the hill loch tumbled down in a landslide, wiped out the village. The disaster took place in the wee hours of morning. At the village there was no sign of human life. The land where the village stood still had turned into a mound of mud. The faces of the deceased were disfigured beyond recognition. What compounded the problem was the presence of a whole crowd and hundreds of vehicles, apparently volunteers from across Pune, who had rushed to the site on hearing the news of the tragedy (Biswas, 2014).

C. Causes of landslides

According to Environmentalists and the Chairman, Madhav Gadgil, Western Ghats Ecology Expert Panel, stated that deforestation causes loosening of the soil and resulting in landslides. Secondly, because of construction of windmill and along with that the access roads are built around the area. The entire constructions are mostly on the hills which disturb the ecology and environment, causing landslides. Gadgil further stated, most of the stone quarries that are illegally constructed, which again disturb the pristine environment. Unfortunately, due to corruption in the government machinery which should check such prohibited works are in hand-in-glove with the perpetrators. Satish Thigale, former head of geology, Pune University said, that any landslide of this scale has two causes, which act together or alone.

1. **The natural cause**: Mountain terrain and heavy rainfall can trigger movement of the soil on a large scale.

2. **Changes made in terrain:** changes made in the terrain for development project can result in such movement of the soil. Thigale further stated- these many casualties show that the government agencies failed to identify the symptoms.

D. Traffic chaos

Mascarehnas Anuradha (2014) in her article captioned "ambulance till midway", stated that at a call at 11 AM 28 ambulances were sent to the state. By then Zilla Parishad dispatched another 30 ambulances and Sassoon Hospital had center set of surgical and orthopedic team along with two ambulances. However, only six ambulances were allowed at the site, said the chief operating officer Dr. D. Shelke.

Other ambulances were stopped 35 km away from the spot. They were awaiting instructions to reach the site. Meanwhile, the huge crowd was already at the site and an array of vehicles had already descended at the spot, leading to 10 km traffic snarl. The ambulances that reached the spot found it difficult to cut through the traffic and carry the injured to the nearest hospitals in Manchar, about 60 km away from Malin village.

E. Madhukar Rao Pichad; Cabinet minister, tribal development

The then tribal development Minister, Sri Madhukar Rao Pichad, said that he would talk to the authorities to evacuate the villages on the hilltop and on hill slopes to prevent such eventualities. There are around 4 to 5 villages that had to be evacuated to prevent any such tragedy.

F. Woman, baby rescued alive after nine hours

More Manoj and Khengre Pawan (2014) reported a woman in her 20s and her six month old baby miraculously escaped the nature's fury as they were rescued a good nine hours after the landslide hit the village. The two were trapped in their house built of thatched roof. The mother was tightly holding the baby in her arms. Their entire house was wrapped in a thick layer of mud; the woman and the child were safely removed and administered with first aid.

The woman was found in the state of shock and was both physically and mentally exhausted. Total 12 Earth movers were pressed into service to remove debris and mud. The affected people were stuck under the mud, reportedly around 200 houses and most are affected. Most relief and rescue operation personnel said that removing dead cattle, people and the shattered houses was a tedious and emotionally challenging task.

G. Hirabai Gare lost nine members of her family

Kulkarni (2014) reported that Gare - a member of the Koli Mahadev tribe community broke down at a mass funeral service at Malin village in Pune. She lost nine members of her family including three children. The National disaster response Force (NDFR) recovered around 70 bodies by August 1, 2014. Names of the identified deceased persons were published in the local newspapers. The disaster management operation by the district administration as well as NDFR was covered by both print and electronic media.

H. NDFR kept a close watch on Bubra River for bodies

Braving the incessant rains, the National Disaster Response Force (NDFR) personnel kept a close watch on Bubra River for the bodies (Kulkarni, 2014). NDFR personnel were deployed along the Bubra River, which runs in the valley in front of Malin village. A total of nine teams, comprising of NDRF personnel were brought to the site of the landslide and resumed operations as soon as they reached the site, and recovered dead bodies of the victims.

I. Suffocation and Poly-trauma caused death

The deputy medical director (Pune Circle) Dr. Chavan and 28 medical officers and another batch of staff nurses were deputed at the site and the post-mortem Centre to facilitate identification of dead bodies to the relatives. It was reported suffocation, poly-trauma and multiple fractures were the cause of death of villagers at Malin.

Dyaneshwar Shelke, chief operating officer of the Maharashtra State emergency medical services, said that nearly 60 ambulances were used to sent injured to the rural hospitals in Ghodegaon, Manchar, Dimbhe, Adhivre. The ambulances were also used to transport the dead bodies to the post-mortem Centre.

J. As villagers flee in panic, no one protect rice paddy fields

Rice cultivation has been the traditional occupation at Malin village. Prasad, (2014) reported several acres of paddy fields, producing good quality rice varieties of "Indrayani" and "Ambe-Mohar", were left unattended at the Malin village, as many families and their relatives died in the landslide. There was no one to look after several paddy fields amounting to heavy losses. Moreover, the survivors were gripped in panic, trauma and psycho-social shock.

K. Kins of victims divided over location of new homes

Most survivors of the landslide disaster expressed fear and apprehension in settling down in the same relatively unsafe terrain. They felt rehabilitation of affected people should be done in safest possible areas and in the safe human habitation. Mr. Zangare, a native of Malin village, who has lost five relatives in Malin landslide, said that the government should allocate homes for the survivors and their families in some relatively urban belt in the adjacent areas to Ghodegaon and Raj guru Nagar. He voiced their demand must be considered by the state government for rehabilitation as he told the Newsline. Tanaji Pote, a 66-year-old, who lost six relatives in the landslide, said he wanted a home not far away from the earlier location as he had to look after the farms. He suggested the government should set up a new Malin village in a safer place.

(b) At local, state and central level attention should be given to preserve ecology, environment by preventing uncontrolled expansions of hydro projects and widening of roads without proper assessment and planning.

(c) Prevention and control unauthorized constructions and encroachments.

(d) Educate local communities and tourists about the impending disasters in Uttarakhand, Himachal and other hilly states.

(e) Encourage research and development in the field of disaster management.

(f) Control and better management of tourist/pilgrim programme and regulated tourist flow in these regions.

Vulnerability of Himalayan region to disasters

Sangevar (2014:214) stated that, considering the present-day scenario of faster pace of industrial growth and development activities in the inaccessible geographical areas, away from urban conglomerates vis a vis growing risk of impending disaster, there is a felt need to have trained human resources in the field of disaster management.

The Himalayan region in India has 9575 glaciers spread over the northern states (Sangameshwar and Shukla 2009, Sangameshwar and Kulkarni, 2011). The existence of glaciers has influence on the natural process in the region. With change in the climate the normal geomorphic processes can be destabilized. Snow avalanches are very common in the Himalayan regions. Snow avalanches can be forecasted in advance to save the lives and properties of people. Rathod (2014) has presented lessons learnt from the disaster episode in Kedarnath.

Lessons Learnt: Uttarakhand Disaster

Preparedness Measures: Registration of pilgrims is very important in major yatras or any event where huge gatherings of people take place. In Maharashtra we have Nashik Mahakumbh mela and every year we have Pandharpur, Tuljapur, Shirdi and Shegaon yatras where huge number of devotees from various parts of Maharashtra and India come together. Computer Software could be developed where pilgrims can register his name and other vital details at multiple entry points where they may be given unique identity number for that Yatra. Only at entry itself one should be given probable period of one's stay in that event and the exit will also be recorded in computer software so that at any particular point of time it would be easy to know the total number of population in that event. The Aadhar linked IT System can be evolved so that only single finger print can get all record and save time for detail entries.

Many officers from the Maharashtra team who worked in the Uttarakhand disaster emphasized that there is a greater need of groups of dedicated and interested officers at District and State level ready to volunteer and work in such disasters as responders on short notice. These motivated, dedicated officers from various departments should be trained and equipped to work in an emergency situation, Yashada can act as a Platform for such forum.

Emergency Response teams should be equipped with communication paraphernalia like satellite phones, Ham radios, Extra mobiles, wireless, laptops and internet dongles and other emergency equipments to function as a mobile control room. Adequate financial powers should be delegated to such team to procure essential items in an emergency situation. Pilgrims and local community should be given safety tips at multiple points about Dos and Don'ts in case of various probable hazards happening in the area of yatras/events. There should be public awareness programme and media campaign designed specifically for prior and during each yatras/events.

There should be predetermined disaster management system as it takes time to prepare orders with last minute planning and issue these orders to concerned personnel in

...imes. Such events should be managed by using emerg... re IRS teams should be informed to be ready in IRS ...y disaster event happens. IRS is very good ca...ent tool to handle such events or disaster situations. ...accountability of everybody is fixed in IRS with clear ...authority. IRS teams should be constituted for each ...aving trained officers. Any big event should be ...ed by proper team formation, team orientation and ...g.

It is essential to Reserve ration quota, medicine, necessary ...ch and rescue equipment and relief material according to ...tion and season should be stored at nearest safe places or strategic locations. Kerosene, ATF oil, Transport system and Electricity restoration units with proper and sufficient equipment should be kept in respective places.

Local Administration should be able to anticipate the needs of first few days of affected population and responders in such emergency situation. Training in the areas of damage, needs assessment and Humanitarian Logistics and Procurement Procedures in Emergency should be provided to all stakeholders. State Government should do Rate contracts for specific material needed at large scale in an emergency and pre-identify and prepare a list of donors of local, state and national level for different relief material. There should be real time coordination with Indian Meteorological Department and early warning systems.

Staff of State EOC, District EOC should be given training and the EOCs should be upgraded. Also GIS mapping should be used in EOCs.

Nodal officers for Army, Air Force and NDRF should be identified and the local/state level disaster authority should be in touch with them. As a preparedness measure, these forces should be taken into confidence while managing an event/yatras prior to probable disaster. Nodal officer should attend their briefings before operations.

Communication failure itself is a big hazard. ... Phones and HAM radios, alternate system of communicate should be already there in such yatras.

Doctors should be trained about their SOP in pro... disaster situations and should have necessary and suffi... medicines at their disposal.

Measures to be taken in Response and Instant Relief

In Disaster situations, when an Executive officer is sent to help and coordinate in the field his personal mobile number shouldn't be published as helpline number over a mass media. Such a publication of personal number on mass media leads to complex situation as he cannot focus on the work assigned to him; hundreds of calls come on such helpline number from the relatives of people stranded/affected to get information. In fact EOC's or temporary control room's number should be published. It is duty of EOC or control room or media center to answer such calls in coordination with field officers.

The State EOC, District EOC and mobile control room or Incident command posts should be activated as per the requirement. The Policy decisions should be taken in coordination with the District and State EOC as such realistic and instant decisions support the machinery in the field for rapid implementation.

Those officers from Maharashtra who worked in Haridwar, Rishikesh and Jolly Grant Airport found that the evacuees needed psychological counseling and social support in such kind of disaster. Evacuees needed emotional and moral support and had to be dealt with very sensitively in such distress time. Vulnerable population like pregnant women, old aged, children etc. needed special attention and care. Many a time language was a major barrier in communication specifically for the people from southern states as they were unable to communicate with the officers working in the disaster sites and camps. The officials need interpreters in such events where different language speaking persons are affected. Thousands of persons evacuated from the affected areas who were from different part of the country were assembling in the railway stations of Rishikesh and Haridwar. It was very difficult to identify people and was a chaotic situation; hence each state's volunteers could set up Help Desk to the victims from specific states. So the officers working in such situation should be given some sort of Reflective jackets and Banners to be identified.

In order to maintain transparent and proper accounts of disbursement of ex-gratia amounts and emergency procurement in such kind of an emergency situations few accounts officer should be part of a team and should be accountable to a higher authority.

Looking at the experiences of SDM Rudraprayag and other officers working in these disaster situations, list of persons available and working at different locations in such disaster situations should be prepared from every possible location and should be published regularly with updates on internet so that panic of the family members and relatives could be minimized. Effective and timely communication can reduce the panic and distress to a great extent.

Rescuers' Safety and Welfare

Logistics arrangement of Air force pilots and state representatives from various states in an emergency was very crucial in Dehradun. Rescue operation volunteer's safety should be given prior importance. Mr. Ajit Arora, SDM of Almora who was deputed at kedarnath valley during operation he lost his life after he swept away in the Mandakini River when he slipped from a wooden bridge.

Coordination Issues

IAG - Inter-Agency Group of NGOs should be formed as a preparedness measure for effective NGO coordination during a disaster. Officers from State EOC, State level officers of Disaster Management division should attend IAG meetings. The NGOs should report to the administration and distribute relief in accordance with the advice of local administration. The NGOs or Trusts should not directly go and distribute relief material in any part as it creates panic and Law and Order problems. The relief distribution should be centralized and it should be under one umbrella under which all resources, man and material should be merged. There should be one command to coordinate response in such an emergency, the officers coming from other states should know with whom he has to coordinate, there should be single point of coordination from the home state.

Social Media Coordination and Management

A revolution in digital communications makes it easier and economical for groups of people to share and work for common purposes. Several central and state government agencies have begun to leverage social media for public awareness and education for Disaster management. Today young people take these new forms for granted; they are increasingly becoming popular and more essential way to deliver public awareness and public education. Social media consists of online tools that allow communicating and networking without any organizational support. Small or large-group broadcasting, knowledge sharing collaboration, multimedia sharing and collective assessment are easily managed, making it possible to experiment to see what works.

District Information Officers should be trained in Disaster Management Information Systems and IRS system should proactively brief the media and press with genuine information through prior approved press notes from appropriate authority. Most importantly during any crisis sensationalisation and politicization of messages should be completely avoided.

Psychosocial Shock and Emotional Experiences of Khillari Earthquake Victims

Earthquakes have been the most devastating natural disasters in the present century. The Marathwada earthquake of September 1993 was one of the worst tragedies that captured the attention of the world. The earthquakes measured 6.5 on the Richter scale and near about 9000 people died and 14,000 people were injured and total sixty seven villages were destroyed completely. It was reported that property worth Rupees 300 crores was destroyed.

Near about 10,000 army personnel were deployed and engaged to comprise as troops, Sappers, engineers and medical units. For the rescue and relief operations a total of 12,000 civic officials were employed in the Khillari earthquake disaster relief and rehabilitation work. The Bombay Psychiatric Society, Sangli Psychiatric Association and Western Zone Psychiatric Society played a significant role in the psychological rehabilitation of the survivors of the earthquake in Latur district, in the State of Maharashtra, India.

1. The psychosocial scenario

Babulkar (2014:208) observed the following emotional expressions of the survivors of Khillari earthquake.

- Shock
- Emotional numbness
- Powerlessness- loss of source of livelihood
- Restlessness- I am unable to do any activity
- Quarrels in the family over property, etc
- Sleep disturbance
- Hopelessness
- Loneliness due to the loss of loved ones
- Negative attitude towards self
- Tendency to consume alcohol
- Always tensed and fearful
- Suicidal tendencies

Disaster affected population need broader range of psychological care in the process of rehabilitation Babhulkar (2014) the following aspects need to be kept in mind while formulating the intervention:

- Understanding their feelings and fears towards disaster and acknowledge their pain

- Pursuing their interests
- Respecting their silence
- Maintaining regular contacts and greeting them and asking them about their welfare
- Sharing their grief and counseling them
- Making them aware of the fact, that they are not to be blamed for the tragedy and they need not feel guilty
- Providing recreation and understanding the value of relaxation

The best conceptualization umbrella of the essential services needed during a disaster was described by Raphael, B. & Middleton, W. (1987) ranging from self-care to medical care as given below:

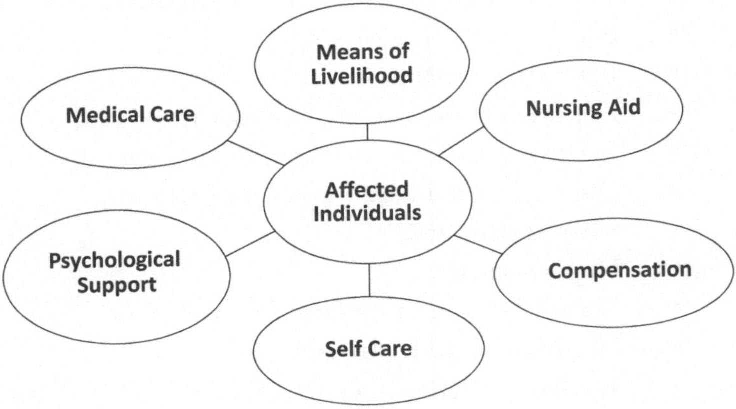

1. Lectures on disaster management

A series of lectures can be organized throughout different semester for students and teachers of colleges and universities on Disaster Management followed by interactive sessions chaired by experts.

2. Exhibitions

Exhibitions can be organized to educate students and teachers of colleges and universities on prevention, preparedness and control over natural and manmade disasters. Experts from the field of disaster management both from national and international NGO's and Government sectors can organize these exhibitions at least twice a year on higher educational institutes.

3. Films and documentaries

Films and Documentaries produced by National Geographic, Discovery Channel and internationally known film and documentary makers, should be screened in the colleges/universities on a regular interval. In fact, teachers of colleges and universities must use these films once in a while to give students a break from their normal academic sessions.

4. Skits, drama and plays

Skits, dramas and plays could be organized in colleges and universities by the management to create awareness about disasters and better prepare for any eventualities.

5. Counseling classes

Students from behavioural sciences may be training in Trauma counseling so that they may volunteer during any disaster situation. Generic educative classes on preparedness, prevention, first aid and management will help students and teachers to mentally prepare themselves to prevent, control and face a disaster for that matter.

6. Field visits

Disaster response and Field interventions should be arranged by colleges and universities to respond to the disaster affected sites and rehabilitation centers, where victims of a given disaster relief, rehabilitation and treatment. This will not only educate the students and teachers about the disaster but also may be of great help in the coordination of relief and rehabilitation work in their area.

7. Role of medical colleges

Whenever there are such disaster situations the medical colleges can place students and faculty members on in disaster affected camps to provide first aid and essential medical care and referral services; to understand health and nutritional issues of the disaster victims. There students can also conduct research and documentation on health, medical and nutritional issues of children, women and the elderly in an affected area.

8. Research

One of the major functions of higher educational institutes is to conduct research on the impact of a disaster on the social, economic and cultural life of people affected by a disaster. The studies should be taken up by a team of experts from social sciences, medical faculties and Health sciences and Disaster Management disciplines, so as to get a holistic understanding of the research problem and specific recommendations for the interventions. Such inter-disciplinary research studies would not only contribute to development of theoretical insights in social sciences, medical and health sciences, but will also is useful to policy makers to plan preventive strategies for various forms of disasters.

9. Debates on peace and communal harmony

Debates and discussions on peace and communal harmony could be organized to sensitize students on manmade disasters, such as riots, wars, stampedes, suicide bomb squads, Naxalism, terrorism and road accidents etc.

Although disaster management is taught as an op subject in development studies, social works, public h sociology, and to some extent as a Masters and diploma some educational institutes however a large number students are unaware of the disaster management. It is henc necessary for the higher educational institutions to create awareness among both teachers and students about prevention and control of disasters.

Role of Educational Institutions

In his preface to a book captioned, "perspective on governance of higher education: issues, concerns and challenges, Dr. Shivaji Rao Kadam, Vice Chancellor, Bharati Vidyapeeth, Pune, has stated that higher education system in India has grown in a remarkable way, particularly in the Post-independence period. The higher education sector in India is considered to be the third largest system in the world, which caters education to approximately 99.54 Lakh students, through 42 Central Universities, 259 state Universities, 130 Deemed-to-be Universities, 65 private Universities and more than 18000 colleges (Kadam, 2010).

Approximately, 4.57 Lakh teachers, demonstrate varied nature of roles as teachers, guides, mentor, administrators and researchers. This enormous growth certainly calls for good governance. However, the figure of colleges and Universities quoted by Kadam in 2010, these figures have gone in the recent past e.g. as of February 2017, there are 789 Universities, 37,204 Colleges and 11,443 Stand-alone institutions in India as per the latest statistics from the University Grants official Website at www.indiaeducation.net/universities.

Nevertheless, the point, we are trying to make here is that the students and teachers of colleges and universities can certainly co-ordinate following activities, under the guidance of administrators to organize following activities and programs on Disaster Management in their campuses.

10. Role of social and development studies students

Much is expected from the students of social work, public health and development planning when it comes to understanding disaster and emergency management and rendering services as well. These students should be exposed to disaster affected sites for relief and rehabilitation work as part of their fieldwork. In addition, they should be given placement assignments with governmental and non-governmental agencies involved in preventive, control and management of disasters.

An exposure to both theory and practice of disaster management would positively educate the students of social work, public health and development planning to understand the problems of victims and survivors of a given disaster and will prepare them to work skillfully for the same after they graduate from their respective educational institutes.

11. Primary research and secondary research

Students from various academic programmes e.g. Masters Degree in various disciplines such as sociology, Anthropology, Social work, Public Health, Political Science, Economics, Development Planning, Disaster Management, Human Resource Management, Law and other allied faculties should be encouraged to carry out primary and secondary research studies on various disaster related topics.

12. M.Phil. and Ph.D.'s

With the growing concerns related to disasters the Educational institutes are encouraging students to take up Disaster Management related issues for their dissertation in M.phil. and Ph.D. programmes. Secondly, a good number of exceptional unpublished M.Phil and Ph.D. thesis have not been published. They are seen on the shelves of libraries, higher educational institutes should encourage students to publish their thesis.

13. Workshops, seminars and Conferences

It is observed that very few educational institutes arrange workshops, seminars and conferences on disaster management and allied issues. Efforts should be made to organize such activities in the colleges and universities.

14. Role of Academic Staff Colleges (ASC)

The noble aim of the ASC is to transform the educators into motivating role models for the young and receptive students with intend to create an equitable and orderly society. The academic staff colleges affiliated to various universities imparts training to teachers and other trainees. These colleges also can organize lectures on disaster management and mitigation related programmes.

15. The department of adult continuing education and extension

Most universities in India have the Department of Adult continuing Education and Extension, which has a network with several colleges, its students and teachers. The said department also has distance education courses, including in-house courses. These departments can play an important role in creating awareness and imparting education on disaster management to educational institutes.

16. Distance learning centers, institutes and universities

The Indira Gandhi Open University (IGNOU) is a central university established by an Act of parliament in 1985. It is the apex distance education institute in the country providing education and training to millions of untrained/undertrained learners through open and distance mode using distance mode and multimedia approach. It caters education to over 4 million students in India and 36 other countries through 21 schools of studies and a network of 67 regional Centre's and around 3000 learner's support center's (Kasturi, 2014). Besides IGNOU there are several other distance educational institutes that can play an important role in creating awareness, spreading education and training modules of disaster management.

17. Department of mass communication

Masters and Ph. D. students of the department of Mass Communications can take up projects to design eco- culturally acceptable modules and strategies to disseminate messages to prevent, control and manage disasters among students and the general public as well.

18. Role of Educational Media and Research Centre (EMRC)

One of the functions of E.M.R.C. is to produce documentaries and films on educational issues. The institute can take up educational programs in disaster management in the larger interest of the Indian society.

19. Role of NSS

Every university in India has a vast network of colleges, with thousands of students associated with the National Service Scheme. The respective colleges assign students volunteers to various community development assignments in the urban slums as well as rural areas. The teachers who organize and manage the projects are dedicated and work on a social cause. It is recommended that the NSS students should be trained about basics of disaster management and they should be exposed to affected sites and areas. Here again the NSS programmes of the colleges and universities have a crucial role to play.

20. Publications and educational awareness material

Higher educational institutes have no dearth of intellectuals and experts in education, publication and training. These experts should carry out research, micro-planning exercises and Participatory Learning Appraisal Studies to develop educational publication to create awareness of disaster prevention and management. Given below are a few suggestion designed by Tribhuvan Robin (2015).

(i) Awareness material for Zilla Parishad and Tribal Ashram schools

Educational experts must collaborate with the Tribal and Rural Development Ministries of GOI and the respective state governments to develop awareness material on disaster prevention, control and management for Zilla Parishad and Tribal Ashram schools in the country. Education regarding the same can be disseminated using:

(i) Folk media- including songs, proverbs, chants, dance forms and dramas etc.

(ii) Traditional Paintings- Traditional paintings could be used to convey messages to a given region or a community.

(iii) Pamphlets and booklets - Design simple pamphlets and booklets in local languages for the common people in the slums, rural and tribal areas. Booklets with less scripts and more pictorial messages could be used to transmit the right kind of message to people in the field of disaster management (Pawar and Robin, 2007).

(iv) Proverbs- proverb too can be used to pass on information to rural masses.

21. Syllabus

Syllabus in disaster management has already been implemented for some disciplines in social sciences. It is necessary to popularize the same and roll out on a larger scale. The objectives in the syllabus may cover the following – (a) Basic conceptual understanding of disasters and its relationships with development, (b) Approaches of Disaster Risk Reduction (DRR) and the relationship between vulnerability, disasters, disaster prevention and risk reduction, (c) Public Health and Psycho-Social Response to Disasters, (d) Prevention and control of Public Health consequences of Disasters, (e) Awareness of Disaster Risk Management and institutional processes in India, (f) Building necessary skills in responding to disasters.

The syllabus may be organised and delivered by a teacher of any discipline as Disaster Management (DM) is multi disciplinary and draws its knowledge base from a range of disciplines.

22. Books

Numerous books have been published on the subject of disaster management; however there are scarcely any books highlighting intervention strategies, case studies and success stories in prevention, control and management of disasters. Educational institutes must make efforts to publish the same.

23. Exhibitions

Public awareness and public education for disaster risk reduction may be organized by periodic exhibitions in different communities. Exhibitions on this subject also should be organized in schools, colleges and universities with the help of experts and event managers.

24. Debates

Debates on this subject should be organized in higher educational institutes so as to create awareness and educate the students as well as teachers. To sum up educational institutes have a great responsibility to educate and train the students in this regard.

25. E-learning

E-learning methodology has developed rapidly over the past decade. Web-based and computer-based teaching and learning with the help of computer DVD, internet access are two effective means of access to collaborative learning. E-learning in disaster management training has been widely studied, and in higher education and service organizations, it has demonstrated that students in online learning have actually performed better than those in face-to-face courses. The main benefits of e-learning, where internet access is available and affordable are: (a) 24/7 flexible access, (b) Abundant online study materials could be uploaded,

(c) Prospect of prominent experts could share knowledge widely, (d) Option of self-paced learning, which accommodates individual requirements, (e) Availability of text, audio and video, to accommodate different learning modalities, (f) Economic and low cost per student.

In e-learning, the theory and practice should remain integrated in the curriculum. These approaches work fine in the curriculum where the contents should be consistent, standard, and emphasis should be given on mastery of skills during the practical exposures.

5

Role of Government and Non-governmenal Organisations

Introduction

India is one of the most disaster prone countries in the world. It has had some of the world's most severe droughts, famines, cyclones, chemical disasters, made air head-on air collisions, rail accidents, road accidents and other man-made disasters. Indian is also one of the most terrorist prone countries (Choudhary, 2014).

In the past India used to accept international aid in responding to disasters. However, after the 2004 Indian oceans tsunami and the Uttarakhand tragedy in 2013, India responded very well without waiting for any assistance from foreign governments, instead deployed its defense personnel, medical teams, disaster experts, ships, helicopters and other resources to tackle the emergency.

This chapter highlights the role of some of the government and non-governmental organizations in prevention and control of disaster. First we may understand some of the government organisations associated with disaster management.

Role of Government Agencies

Disaster Management Act, 2005 (GoI, 2005)

The Act lays down institutional, legal, financial and coordination mechanisms at the national, state, district and local levels. These institutions are not parallel structures and work in close harmony. The new institutional framework is expected to usher in a paradigm shift in DM from relief centric approach to a proactive regime that lays greater emphasis on preparedness, prevention and mitigation.

Institutional Framework under the DM Act 2005

National Disaster Management Authority (NDMA)

The NDMA, as the apex body for disaster management, is headed by the Prime Minister and has the responsibility for laying down policies, plans and guidelines for DM. The apex body coordinates their enforcement and implementation of various policies and programmes for ensuring timely and effective response to disasters. The guidelines assist the Central Ministries, Departments and States to formulate their respective DM plans. It approves the National Disaster Management and DMs plans of the Central Ministries and Departments. It takes such other measures as it may consider necessary such as for the prevention of disasters, mitigation, preparedness, capacity building and for dealing with an impending and hostile disaster situation the body always remains vigilant. The Central ministries/departments and state governments extends necessary cooperation and assistance to NDMA for carrying out its mandate and oversees the provision and application of funds for mitigation and preparedness measures. The NDMA has the power to authorize the departments or authorities concerned, to make emergency procurement of provisions or materials for rescue and relief in a threatening disaster situation or disaster. The general superintendence, direction and control of National Disaster Response Force (NDRF) are vested in and are exercised by the NDMA. The National Institute of Disaster Management (NIDM) works within the framework of broad policies and guidelines laid down by NDMA.

The NDMA is mandated to deal with all types of disasters, natural or man-made. Whereas, such other emergencies including those requiring close involvement of the security forces and/or intelligence agencies such as terrorism (counterinsurgency), law and order situation, serial bomb blasts, hijacking, air accidents, Chemical, Biological, Radiological and Nuclear (CBRN) weapons systems, mine disasters, ports and harbor emergencies, forest fires, oilfield fires, and oil spills will continue to be handled by the existing mechanism i.e., National Crisis Management Committee.

The NDMA may, however, formulate guidelines and facilitate training in preparedness activities in respect of, Chemical, Biological, Radiological and Nuclear (CBRN) emergencies. Crosscutting themes like medical and public health preparedness, psychosocial care in trauma, community-based disaster preparedness, information and communication technology, training, community awareness programmes etc. for natural and man-made disasters will also engage the attention of NDMA in the partnership with other concerned stakeholders. Resources are available with the disaster management authorities at all level, which are capable of discharging emergency support functions, will be made applicable to the nodal ministries/agencies dealing with the emergencies at times of impending disasters.

The National Executive Committee

The National Executive Committee (NEC) comprises of the Union Home Secretary as the chairperson, and the secretaries to the GOI In the Ministries/Departments of Agriculture, Atomic Energy, Defense, Drinking Water Supply, Environment and Forests, Finance (Expenditure), Health, Power, Rural Development, Science and Technology, Space, Telecommunications, Urban Development and the Chiefs of Integrated Defense Staff are the Committee members. Secretaries in the Ministry of External Affairs, Earth Sciences, Human Resource Development, Mines, Shipping, Road Transport and Highways and the secretary of the NDMA will be special invitees to the meetings of the NEC.

The NEC is the executive committee of the NDMA, and is mandated to assist the NDMA in the discharge of its functions and also ensure compliance of the directions issued by the Central government. The NEC is to coordinate the responses in the event of any threatening disaster situation. It will prepare the National Plan for Disaster Management based on the National Policy on Disaster Management. The NEC will monitor the implementation of guidelines issued by the NDMA. It will also perform such other functions as may be prescribed by the Central government in consultation with the NDMA.

State Disaster Management Authority (SDMA)

At the state level, the SDMA, headed by the Chief Minister, which lay down policies and plans for DM in the state. It will, inter alia approved the state plan in accordance with the guidelines laid down by the NDMA, coordinate the limitation of the State plan, recommend provision of funds for mitigation and preparedness measures and review the developmental plans of the different departments of the state to ensure integration of prevention, preparedness and mitigation measures.

The State government constituted a State Executive Committee (SEC) to assist the SDMA in the performance of its functions. The SEC headed by the Chief Secretary to the state government and coordinates and monitors the implementation of the National Policy, National Plan, and the State Plan. The SEC also provides information to the NDMA relating to different aspects of DM.

District Disaster Management Authority (DDMA)

The DDMA is headed by the district collector, deputy commissioner or district Magistrate as the case may be, with the elected representative of the local authority as co-chairperson. DDMA acts as the planning, coordinating and implementing body for DM at the district level and take all necessary measures for the purposes of DM in accordance with the guidelines laid down by the NDMA and SDMA. It inter alia prepares the district DM plan for the district and monitors the implementation of the National Policy, the State

Policy, the National Plan, State Plan, and the District Plan. The DDMA also ensures that the guidelines for prevention, mitigation, preparedness and response measures lay down by the NDMA and the SDMA are followed by all departments of the state government at the district level and the local authorities of the district.

Local Authorities

For the purpose of this policy, local authorities include Panchayati Raj Institutions (PRI), Municipalities, District and Cantonments Boards and Town Planning Authorities which control and manage civic services. These bodies ensure capacity building of their officers and employees for managing disasters, carry out relief work, rehabilitation and reconstruction activities in the affected areas and prepare DM plans in consonance with guidelines of the NDMA, SDMAs and DDMAs. Reportedly specific institutional framework for dealing with disaster management issues in mega cities are put in place.

National Institute of Disaster Management

The NIDM, in partnership with other research institutions has the capacity development as one of its major responsibilities, along with training, research, documentation and development of a national level information base. It networks with other knowledge-based institutions and function within the broad policies and guidelines laid down by the NDMA. It organizes training of trainers, DM officials and other stakeholders. The NIDM strives to emerge as a 'Centre of Excellence' in the field of disaster management.

National Disaster Response Force (NDRF)

For the purpose of specialized response to a threatening disaster situation all disasters/emergencies both natural and man-made such as those of Chemical, Biological, Radiological and Nuclear (CBRN) origin, Disaster Management Act, 2005 has mandated the constitution of a National Disaster Response Force (NDRF). The general superintendents, direction and control of this force shall be vested on and exercised by the NDMA. The command and supervision of the force shall be delegated to an officer to be appointed by the Central government as the Director General of Civil Defense and National Disaster Response Force. Presently, the NDRF comprises 10 battalions and further expansion may be considered in due course. These battalions have been positioned at different locations as per the threat perception. NDRF units will maintain closed liaison with the designated state governments and will be available to them in the event of any serious threatening disaster situation. Handling of natural disasters rests with the NDRF battalions and they are also equipped and trained to respond to situations arising out of Chemical, Biological, Radiological and Nuclear emergencies. Training centre set up by respective paramilitary forces to train personnel from NDRF battalions of respective forces and also made the training requirement of State/UT Disaster Response Forces. The NDRF units also impart basic training to all the stakeholders identified by the state governments in their respective locations. Further, a National Academy is being said to provide training for trainers in disaster management and to meet related national and international commitments.

Experience in major disasters in the last decade has clearly established the need for pre-positioning of some essential reserves at crucial locations, including some for the high altitude areas. These reserves are intended to augment the resources at the state-level. Mitigation reserves are placed at the disposal of National Disaster Response Force for enhancing their emergency responding Capabilities for assisting the state governments during a disaster or disaster like situation.

Existing Institutional Arrangements

The Cabinet Committee on Management of Natural Calamities (CCMNC) and the Cabinet Committee on Security (CCS)

The CCMNC had been constituted to oversee all aspects relating to the management of natural calamities including an assessment of the situation and identification of measures and programs considered necessary to reduce its impact, monitor and suggest long-term measures for prevention of such calamities formulate and recommend programs for public awareness for building up society's resilience to them. The Cabinet Committee on Security (CCS) deals with issues related to the defense of the country, law and order and internal security, policy matters concerning foreign affairs that have internal or external security implications and economic and political issues impinging on national-security.

Role of Government Organization in Disaster Management

The governments have a prime responsibility for managing disasters and providing relief and rehabilitation services to the affected population. An integrated disaster management mechanism exists within government framework. The essential responsibility of disaster management goes with the state government where the disaster has occurred. The central government supplements their efforts in dealing with disaster response. There is an institutional arrangement at the national, state, district and sub-district levels to cope with emergency situations. A national contingency action plan exists for ensuring emergency systems in the wake of disasters in the national state and district level. The state governments have relief manuals and codes, which lay down the procedures and powers for emergency management and provisions for relief.

The national preparations and planning comprise of a cabinet committee on natural disaster management. The group is chaired by the cabinet secretary. A central relief commissioner in the ministry of agriculture effects disaster relief coordination. Each state government has a relief commissioner and state cabinet level coordination committee. At the district level, the district collector presides over the Relief Committee, which includes people's representatives. At the district level role of local self-government institutions assumes greater importance in disaster management as they are the first responders in emergencies. A Calamity Relief fund is allocated to each state on an annual basis, 70% of which is contributed by central government.

National Disaster Management Authority

Preparatory Phase: During this phase several functions are involved such as Create NDMA, Allocate Funds, Create Legal Framework, Create Resources and Deploy Nodes, Plan Training Policies, Create Communications, Deploy Warning Systems, Conduct Pre-disaster surveys.

Execution Phase: this phase includes - Receive issue warnings, direct observer to take immediate feedback, Allocate funds and deploy coordinate resources, Coordinate with international and regional agencies, execute accountability.

Post Disaster Phase: this phase include – Recreating the used funds for next likely disasters, correct the system and strengthens the reforms, Evaluate the damage and offer help to the state for reconstruction and rehabilitation and undertake further development activities.

State Disaster Management Authority

Preparatory Phase: In this phase various activities such as Create organization, set aside funds at all levels, conduct training, create resources and allocate them, work out legal framework within the national framework, deploy warning systems, work out risk assessment, work out mitigation options, coordinate with the NDMA and the district authority are involved.

Execution Phase: at this stage involves issue warning; execute mitigation plans by deploying resources, co-ordinate with NDMA, estimate damages.

Post Disaster Phase: At this stage re-workout risk assessment and relay mitigation plans, undertake fresh reconstruction and development activities at the earliest carry out accounting funds, strengthens warning systems, reassess training and education needs in consonance with the national of planned scheme in each state basically to meet the requirements for strengthening communica emergency control rooms, thereby improving coord and response to disasters.

Role of International Agencies

All countries in the world today are experiencing some form of newer drastic effect of climate change and natural disaster. Increasingly the greenhouse gas emission continues to rise and currently reports suggest now 50 percent higher than their level in 1990. Moreover, global warming is resulting in deep seeded alteration to our climate and ecological system, which poses irreversible negative consequences if immediate actions are delayed. Annually the average losses from the natural disasters such as earthquakes, tsunamis, floods, and tropical cyclones amounts to hundreds of billions of dollars, that necessitates an huge investment of US $6 billion per annum in disaster risk management only. The goal aims to mobilize $100 billion annually by 2020 to address the needs of developing countries and help mitigate climate-related disasters (UNDP, 2018).

Apposite importance is given on developing countries to assist in lessening the climate-related disaster as per the Goal 13: Climate Action in United Nations Sustainable Development Goals. Disaster threat and planning should be given adequate importance on the development agenda since there are direct association between disasters and development. Universally it is accepted that disaster can lead to destruction of development gains at the same time there are silence discussion and debates on the role that diverse approaches play in the development that creates and increase the risk of vulnerabilities. Preplanned reduction of disaster risks in terms of prevention, preparedness, developing early warning systems for predictable emergencies like storms, cyclones, floods etc. helps to protect both human and economic losses. Disaster risk reduction and resilience requires more central consideration in the present time development agenda the UN response will be coordinated by the UN office for the Coordination of Humanitarian Affairs (UN-OCHA), by deploying the UN Disaster Assessment and Coordination (UNDAC) team, in response to a request by the affected country's government.

6. World Bank

Since the last decade, the World Bank has emerged as the world leader in disaster risk management by supporting affected countries to assess exposure to disaster risks and address the impact. Particularly since 1980, the World Bank has approved more than 500 projects related to disaster management, dealing with both disaster mitigation as well as reconstruction project, amounting to more than US$ 40 billion. These projects have taken place all over the world, in countries such as Argentina, Bangladesh, Columbia, Haiti, India, Mexico, Turkey and Vietnam. Prevention and mitigation projects include forest fire prevention measures, such as early warning measures and education campaigns; early warning systems for hurricanes; flood prevention mechanism (for example shore protection, terracing, etc.); and earthquake prone construction.

In a joint venture with the Columbia University under the umbrella of Prevention Consortium the World Bank has established a Global Risk Analysis of Natural Disaster Hotspots. According to World Bank (2018) if the countries act decisively, they can save human lives and property. But many low income countries lack the expertise, tools and instruments to protect and prevent the potential impacts of disasters into their investment decisions.

7. European Union

In 2001, the EU adopted Community Mechanism for Civil Protection, to facilitate cooperation in the event of major emergencies requiring urgent response actions. The European Commission's Civil Protection and Humanitarian Aid Operations Department initiated the Emergency Response Coordination Centre (ERCC) which was set up to support with the coordinated and faster response to disasters both inside and outside Europe by means of resources from the countries participating in the EU Civil Protection Mechanism. The ERCC has the capability to deal with several concurrent emergencies in different time zones, around-the-clock; it is a coordination center facilitating a rational European response at the time of disaster by helping to curtail avoidable and costly duplication of services and efforts.

This also applies to situations where there may be an immediate threat as well. The heart of the mechanism is the Monitoring and Information Centre (MIC), Part of the European Commission's Directorate General for Humanitarian Aid and Civil Protection. Accessible 24 hours a day, it gives countries access to one stop shop of civil protections available amongst all the participating States. Any country outside or inside the union affected by a major disaster can make an appeal for assistance through the MIC. It acts as a communication hub, and provides useful and updated information on the actual status of an ongoing emergency. It collects and analyses instantaneous data on disasters, monitors emergencies, prepares plans for the deployment of experts, allocating teams and equipment, and works with Member States to map available assets and coordinate the EU's disaster response efforts by matching offers of assistance to the needs of the disaster-stricken country. The ERCC also supports a wide range of prevention and preparedness activities, from awareness-building to field exercises generating emergency response.

Response of Some Countries

Several countries and their respective governments come forward to support disaster rescue, relief and rehabilitation programs. Given below are few noteworthy initiatives in some selected countries.

1. **Australia:** Natural disasters are a part of life in Australia. Heat waves have killed more Australians than any other type of natural disaster in the 20th century. Australia's

emergency management processes embraced the concept of prepared community and the government agency is foremost in achieving this is Emergency Management Australia.

2. **Canada:** Public Safety Canada is Canada's national emergency management agency. Each province is required to have both legislation for dealing with emergencies, and provincial emergency management agencies, typically called "Emergency Measures Organizations" (EMO). The Public Safety Canada coordinates and supports the efforts of federal organizations as well as other levels of government, first responders, community groups, the private sector, and other nations. The Public Safety and Emergency Preparedness Act 2005 define the powers, duties and functions of Public Safety and emergency preparedness in the document. Other acts are specific to individual fields such as corrections, law enforcement and national security.

3. **Germany:** in Germany the Federal Government controls the German Katastrophenschutz (Disaster Relief), the Technicsches Hilfswerk (Federal Agency of Technical Relief, THW), and the Zivilschutz (Civil Protection) programs. Local Fire Department units, the German Armed Forces (Bundeswehr) the German Federal police and the 16 State police forces (Landerpolizeii) are also deployed during disaster relief operations. The private organizations in Germany which also deals with emergency relief are the German Red Cross, Johanniter-Unfall-Hilfe (the German equally violent of the St John ambulance), the Malteser-Hilfsdient, and the Aebeiter-Samariter-Bund. There is program of study at the University of Bonn leading to a degree "Master and Disaster Prevention and Risk Governance".

4. **India:** The Protective Wall built on the shore of the coastal town of Kalapakkam, in the aftermath of the 2004 Indian

Ocean Quake. Emergency management in India handled by the National Disaster Management Authority. India, (Ministry of Home Affairs). Recently, emphasis has fted from response and recovery strategy to risk manag and reduction, and also from a government cent approach to decentralized community participation. T Indian Army also plays an important role in the rescue/ recovery operations after a disaster. The Aniruddha's Academy of Disaster Management (AADM) is a non-profit organization in Mumbai, India with disaster management as its principal objective engaged in training, rescue operation and education programmes in Disaster Management for various target audience.

5. **New Zealand:** New Zealand Civil Defense Emergency Management is well a well know initiative in the country. In New Zealand, depending on the scope of the emergency/disaster, the responsibility may be handled either at the local or national level. Within each region, local governments are organized into 16 Defense Emergency Management Groups (DEMGs). Central government has the authority to coordinate the response through the National Crisis Management Centre (NCMC), operated by the Ministry of Civil Defense and Emergency Management (MCDEM).

6. **Pakistan:** Disaster management and Pakistan revolves around flood disasters focusing on rescue and relief. There is a shortage of knowledge and information about hazard identification, risk assessment and management, and disaster preparedness. Disaster management, development planning and environmental management institutions operate in isolation with no integrated linking; there is no central authority for integrated disaster management. The Disaster Risk Management Society is established in the Government College University under the supervision of the Department of Geography which is a public research university located in the downtown, Lahore.

7. **Russia:** Russian President Boris Yeltsin established the Ministry of the Russian Federation for Affairs for Civil Defense, Emergencies and Elimination of Consequences of Natural Disasters also known as The Ministry of Emergency Situations or internationally as EMERCOM (derived from "Emergency Control Ministry") in 1994. In Russia, The Ministry of Emergency Situations (EMERCOM) is engaged in firefighting, civil defense, and search and rescue after both natural and human made disasters. According to an EMERCOM publication, the Ministry is an agency of Federal Executive Power with the following tasks:
   - Managing Civil Defense, search and rescue Service in Russia;
   - Providing support and further development of the Russian System of Disaster Management (RSDM);
   - Directing activities aimed at eliminating the consequences of large-scale disasters, catastrophes and other emergencies;
   - Supervising the use of finance resources allocated to the Government for disaster management and response;
   - Organizing the training of the population, and governing agencies and the RSDM forces for disaster management and response;
   - Organizing international cooperation in the fields of the Ministry's competency.
8. **Somalia:** The Federal Government of Somalia announced in 2013 the Cabinet's approval draft legislation of a new Somalia Disaster Management Agency (SDMA) which had originally been proposed by the Ministry of Interior. According to the Prime Minister's media office, the SDMA will lead and coordinate the government's response to the various natural disasters. It is part of a broader effort by the federal authorities to re-establish national institutions.

9. **The Netherlands:** The Ministry of Interior and Kingdom Relations of Nederland is responsible for home affairs, the civil services, Intelligence services and relations with other countries in the kingdom of the Netherlands. The emergency preparedness and emergency management on a national level and operates a national crisis Centre (NCC). The country is divided into 25 safety regions each covered by three emergency services: police, fire department and ambulance. All regions operate according to the Coordinated Regional Incident Management System. Other services, such as the Ministry of Defense, water boats and risk management of the state have an active role in the emergency management process.
10. **United Kingdom:** The Emergency response recovery guidance endeavored to institute best practice based on lessons learnt and recognized from responding to emergencies both in the UK and internationally (GOV.UK, 2013). The 2000 fuel protests and severe flooding that year, as well as the outbreak of foot-and-mouth disease in the United Kingdom in 2001 caused a crisis in British agriculture and tourism. Then the United Kingdom passed the Civil Contingencies Act (CCA). The CCA defined some organizations as category one and two responders, setting responsibilities regarding emergency preparedness and response. It is managed by the Civil Contingencies Secretariat Regional Resilience Forums and local authorities.

    Disaster management training is generally conducted at local level, and it consolidated to professional courses that can be taken at the Emergency Planning College. Diplomas and graduate and postgraduate qualifications can be gained at universities throughout the country. The Institute of Emergency Management is a charity, established in 1996, dividing consulting services for the government, media and commercial sectors. There is a consultation report which summarizes the response to the March/April 2009 emergency response and recovery consultation and outlines their response.

11. **United States:** In USA the Federal Emergency Management Agency (FEMA) Administrator provide a monthly report on the Disaster Relief Fund (DRF), which includes a funding summary, Disaster Relief Fund - funding activities by state and event, a outline of the financial support for the catastrophic events, and an estimate funds for future. The FEMA is an agency of the US Department of Homeland Security, initially created by Presidential Reorganization Plan No. 3 of 1978 and implemented by two Executive Orders on April 1, 1979. Through the DRF, FEMA can fund authorized Federal disaster support activities as well as eligible State, territorial, tribal, and local actions, such as providing emergency protection and debris removal. Disaster management in the United States has utilized the functional all hazards approach for over 20 years, in which managers develop processes (such as communication and warning or sheltering) rather than developing single hazard/thread focused plans (example a tornado plan). Processes are then mapped to specific hazards/threats, with the manager looking for overlaps and conflicts between processes.

Role of Non-Government Organization's in Disaster Management

A non-government organization has been defined as any non-profit, voluntary citizen's group, which organized on a local, national or international level. The role of non-government organizations are the most effective alternative means of achieving an efficient communication link between the disaster management agencies in the affected community. Different type of NGOs are already contributing in disaster management at advocacy level as well as grass root levels; in preparedness, relief, rescue, rehabilitation, reconstruction and also in monitoring and feedback. In disaster situations, a quick rescue and relief mission is inevitable; however considerable damage to property and life can be minimized, if proper pre-disaster interventions are planned and implemented. The NGOs could significantly contribute to the overall disaster management of the region. Currently the civil society organizations enjoy a conducive and favorable atmosphere in the country in terms of their participation in various social and development programmes. Many NGOs have initiated various activities in the areas of social care, public health, and disaster management. Some of the leading NGOs like OXFARM (India) trust, CASA, CARE-India, Ramkrishna Mission, DMI, etc. have been actively engaged in responding to almost every disaster situation in the country with timely and effective relief operations.

Importance of NGOs Contribution in Disaster Management

1. The greater degree of autonomy, flexibility of the NGOs in the functioning and their regular contact with the people residing in remote disaster prone areas and their involvement during the times of disaster and post disaster activities can immensely help in the effective intervention in disaster management.
2. Many NGOs have demonstrated an ability to reach out to marginalized, economically and socially backward people in the community. They also innovatively and democratically work in the inaccessible areas which may be otherwise difficult for official agencies.
3. Many NGOs play advocacy role and represent the poorer people with close links with communities. The NGOs are also knowledgeable about the local communities and skilled in generating community participation and involvement in the development programmes.
4. The ranges of resources of NGOs are largely additional; they complement the developmental and reconstructive initiatives of the nation. They can help make the development process more accountable, transparent and participatory.

Based on the identified types of NGOs and their capabilities, organized action of NGOs can be very useful in disaster management. In India, the types of roles and responses to situations of disasters by the NGOs can be broadly classified in the following categories:

(a) The main response of NGOs is to provide material relief and rescue operations during the times of disaster including medical relief, social services and public health interventions.

(b) Often the post disaster situations follows a longer period of rehabilitation and reconstruction activities of the physical infrastructure like roads, houses, community buildings, drinking water facilities, continuation of medical and psychosocial support and interventions. In some instances, some financial aid and other assistance provided to affected people to establish their traditional economic pursuits. In these long drawn processes the local NGOs can play very vital and crucial roles.

(c) The initial responses of local NGOs during a calamity are in the form of rescue and material relief; in instances where other activities like reconstruction of houses, etc. are undertaken, they are usually dependent on support from the larger relief agencies and international aid.

(d) Most of the larger Indian NGOs, which are not located in the disaster prone areas, withdraw after the initial phases of relief and reconstruction, while only a few prolong their intervention in the areas for restarting some developmental activities. The Government support is also restricted to relief and rehabilitation. Whereas only a few voluntary agencies stay back in the disaster prone areas for disaster mitigation, long-term development of the people of the area and especially for disaster preparedness before the next disaster strikes. This approach, till date, can be seen only in a few rare exceptions.

(e) The Local NGOs, who also participate in relief and reconstruction activities during times of disasters, revert back to their usual pre-disaster activities from the initial phase.

The below mentioned figure indicates NGOs and Disaster management Cycle, the level of interventions and phase wise role and strategies of non-government organizations in disaster management.

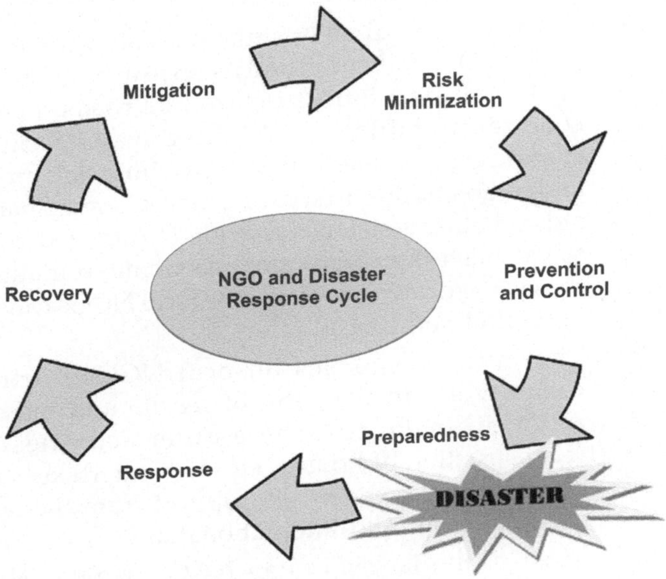

Fig. 5.1: NGOs and Disaster Response Cycle

Local Self-help Groups and NGOs

Preparatory Phase: the role of Self help groups in disaster management and resilience may be an effective strategy. Self-Help Groups are informal associations of people who choose to come together to find ways to improve their difficult situation and living conditions. They help to build Social Capital among the affected, marginalized and poor; especially they develop the local level self-help groups to help themselves. Various specific activities may be undertaken in this direction such as train at individual and community level, create self-help groups and coordinate with the tehsil authorities, keep rescue and relief material under control, identify and confirm custodians, learn about warning systems and area mitigation plans, keep minimum safety levels during all situation including special occasions, make an upgrade mitigation plans at institutional levels and create informal organization's to react during disasters, follow legal and development norms at all times.

Execution Phase: The execution (or implementation) of the intervention is the phase in which the plan designed in the prior phases of the intervention is put into action. The purpose of execution phase is to deliver the expected deliverable and other direct outputs. In this phase various indicators are as: (a) follow warnings and instructions on evacuation; (b) conduct immediate rescue and relief from within the community resources before the formal organization takes control; (c) help the formal organizations in various rescue and relief duties; (d) help identify and dispose the dead and safeguard property and lives; (e) help and distribution of relief material from the authorities; (f) motivate fellow citizens to overcome grief; (g) follow accounting systems; (h) rendered help in running relief camps.

Post Disaster Phase: This phase includes (a) follow governments instructions regarding receiving of compensation and aid honestly; (b) follow revise development norms; (c) upgrade individual, family and institutional level disaster preparedness; (d) learning from the past experiences; (e) report honestly about the damage and avoid over claiming; (f) maintain and upgrade NGOs records; (g) continue to spread awareness.

The NGOs are the most effective means of achieving an efficient and timely communication link between the disaster management agencies and the affected community. For effective disaster mitigation NGOs should maintain proper coordination with government agencies and in implementing essential activities, they should avoid duplication and overlapping of activities and wastage of resources, money and time.

The Government and Non-governmental organizations both may contribute in disaster response, recovery and mitigation, Risk reeducation, prevention and preparedness in disaster management situation (Fig. NGOs and Disaster Response Cycle). Both organizations share common objectives in disaster management and hence, with the help of both these agencies and their machinery it may be possible to turn a disaster into opportunity.

6

Public Health and Social Work Response in Disaster Management

Public Health Responses in Disaster Management

Public health interventions have many parallel with disaster management and mitigation in relation to overall goals of rescue, rehabilitation, treatment, intervention and many operational modalities. The public health professionals are one of major emergency management (EM) multidisciplinary team which strives to protect the community from crisis by means of organizational and science-based interventional strategies. The medical and public health approach addresses threats to human well-being, and outlines specific tools that health and disaster management need to share in order to improve their potential collaboration toward better population outcome in disasters. Public health professional may proficiently respond in the disaster management cycle which may consists of a number of essential roles, such as warning/evacuation, relief and rescue, providing immediate assistance, assessing damage, providing medical care, mental health support, continuing assistance and the immediate restoration of infrastructure. The main objectives of disaster response would be to offer instantaneous assistance to maintain life, treat injuries, improve health and provide psychosocial support and mental health of the affected population. Further specific assistance may range from providing definite but limited aid such as assistance with transport to health facilities, temporary shelter and food. They may assist government agencies and other civil society organization in the response phase by assisting in meeting the basic needs of the people until more lasting and sustainable solutions are instituted.

However, both public health and disaster management are multi-disciplinary in their scientific understandings, while public health as a discipline developed much advanced than the disaster management in developing its own scientific disciplines. In spite of numerous well-known values as well as having many similar operational characteristics, public health and disaster management as a field of study and intervention have mostly failed to share their tools and personnel for collaborative response in the emergency situations. However, public health authorities could have definitive and virtual roles and responsibilities of entire health sector and primary policy makers and implementer of health care. Hospitals and health departments are accountable for a large variety of health care services and activities, often may be organized into various critical and essential services such as maternal and child health, epidemiologic services, disease control and prevention, food and water safety, laboratory services, investigations, environmental health services, occupational safety, licensing of health care practitioners, maintaining vital records, promoting community health awareness and health education. As per the Disaster Management Act, 2005 of India, it is now compulsory for public hospitals in India to prepare a disaster management plan. Additionally, health departments are required to construct and operate a jurisdictional health sector disaster plan to help improve, collaborate and interact within the various parts of the health sector during emergencies, as well as interaction between the health sector and other key stakeholders in disaster management programme.

Disaster Response

Disaster response is known as the second stage of the disaster management cycle which consists of a number of steps such as (a) warning and evacuation; (b) search and rescue; (c) providing immediate assistance; (d) assessing damage; (e) continuing assistance; (f) immediate restoration of infrastructure. The aim of disaster response is to provide immediate assistance to maintain life, improve health, mental health and support the morale of the affected population. The foremost responsibility to address these urgent needs and respond to a disaster innately remains with the government or governments of the same territory where the disaster has struck. Moreover, as discussed earlier the humanitarian organizations often respond proactively and strongly in the disaster management cycle, predominantly in low and middle income countries where the government lacks the resources to respond adequately to the needs of the affected.

An effective emergency response and recovery guidance plan may refer to decisions and actions taken in accordance with the premeditated, planned and operational objectives defined by disaster affected responders so that they could return to normal lives. In most crisis situations it is expected to be comparatively short and to last for a matter of hours or days, therefore quick implementation of preparations for collaboration, co-ordination and communication are very significant. Disaster management and response includes the effort to deal not only with the direct effects of the tragedy itself, e.g. rescuing individuals providing first aid/medical aid, fighting fires, but also the indirect effects such as interruption, social media interest.

The following are universal objectives that the social and health care professionals may be required to be engaged in while in disaster situations:

- Saving and protecting lives of human;
- Relief and rescue;

- Alleviating human suffering;
- Controlling disaster – prevention of escalation, spread and mitigating impacts;
- Providing warning, advice, information to the public;
- Protecting the public health and safety personnel involved in response;
- Protection of the environment;
- Protecting property in realistic ways;
- Maintaining or restoring critical activities;
- Promoting and facilitating self-help in affected communities;
- Supporting the recuperation of the community
- Organize humanitarian assistance, economic, infrastructure and environmental supports;
- Facilitating investigations, inquiries and documentation;
- Evaluating disaster response and recovery efforts and initiatives;
- Identifying and taking corrective action to implement lessons learnt.

Social Work Intervention during Disaster

The Social work profession has defined disasters mainly in terms of the psychosocial impact of natural and technical risks. The professional social workers have been essentially concerned with issues pertaining to disaster such as prevention of extreme disturbances during disaster, impacts of disaster at multiple levels of systemic study and accessibility of equitable services to vulnerable populations e.g. children, women, aged and marginalized people.

Before getting into understanding the role of social work professionals and their interventions in disaster management, it is necessary to discuss the concepts and definition of social work. A common man views social work as a process or action taken by an individual, activist, social worker, a religious or secular trust, an NGO or a development agency to help people with problems or various needs.

Some people associate social work with distribution of stationary, clothes, blankets, tents, medicine, and food to the poor. Similarly some believe in the participatory development approach of involving the community in planning, implementation, monitoring, follow-up and evaluation of development programs or initiatives. Well, there is a lot of debate on charity, social work and participatory sustainable development. Given this background it is pertinent to understand the concept and definition of social work from an academic and scientific perspective.

Definitions and Concepts in Social Work

Ferzana, B. (2011) in her book captioned "Concepts of Social Work Practice" stated that social work may be defined as an art, science, a profession that helps people to solve personal, groups (families) and community problems and relationships through social work methods such as Case Work, Group Work, Community Organization, Social Welfare Administration, Social Work Research and Social Action. The major focus is on reducing problems in human relationships and on enriching living through improved interaction.

According to the International Federation of Social Workers, "Social Work bases its methodology on a systematic body of evidence-based knowledge derived from research and practice evaluation, including local and indigenous knowledge specific to its context. It recognizes the complexity of interactions between human beings and their environment, and the capacity of people both to be affected by or to alter the multiple influences upon them including bio-psycho-social factors. The social work profession draws on theories of human development, social theory and social systems to analyze complex situations and to facilitate individual, organizational, social and cultural changes.

A popular definition of social work that appeared in the curriculum study, sponsored by the Council on Social Work Education: "social work seeks to enhance social functioning of individuals, individually and in group, by activities focused upon their social relationships which constitute interaction between man and environment." These activities can be grouped into three functions:

(i) Restoration of impaired capacity

(ii) Provision of individual and social resources; and

(iii) Prevention of social dysfunction

Principles of Social Work

It is also necessary to discuss the principles of social work at this juncture. Ferzana (2010) writes social work principles are guiding assertions of statements that have come from experience and research. The objectives of social work can be fulfilled only within the framework of principles which are guiding force for social work practice. It is pertinent to note the following principles of social work as described by Konopa and Lindeman (1958).

(i) The social workers goal is to enable clients or group members on group as a whole to move towards greater independence and capacity for help.

(ii) The social workers must use the scientific method to prepare for action; fact-finding (observation), analysis and diagnosis in relation to the individual, group and the social environment.

(iii) The social worker must built purposeful relationships: this means a conscious focus on the needs of the clients, group members and communities.

(iv) The social worker must use himself/herself consciously. This includes self-knowledge indiscipline in relationship but without the loss of warmth and genuineness.

(v) The social worker must understand the origin of his own value system and be able to handle it in relation to the value system of others.

(vi) The social worker must accept people as they are. This involves deeper understanding of his/her clients.

(vii) He/she must allow people to develop their own pace and to choose their own point of departure, without immediately imposing outside demands. However, he/she has the responsibility for stimulating change.

(viii) Because of his/her infinite respect for the individual, every social worker must help each individual to feel that he/she is important and unique person, who I. can contribute in some measure to the whole of society or to a part of it.

Clarke has described principles of social work as follows:

(i) All individuals have an inner and outer life which interacts. How people feel about their situation is perhaps more important than the situation itself.

(ii) All behaviors have a history, the theory of determinism in psychic life.

(iii) Most of the behavior is not intellectually, but emotionally motivated and is symptomatic of emotional needs.

(iv) The family is a unit of interacting personalities and has the most important effects of any institution upon the degree of personality integration.

(v) Treatment of emotional difficulties is facilitated by understanding the history of the onset of the disturbances which may occur in infancy or early childhood.

(vi) Treatment of emotional problems can be effective only in case of the person who is emotionally disturbed, wants to improve it.

Major Activities in the Field of Social Work

Ferzana (2010) has classified 13 activities in the field of social work. These are as below:

Methods of Social Work in Disaster Management

It is imperative to understand the relevance of methods and practice of social work in disaster management. Social work as a discipline of social science has a lot to offer in prevention, control and management of various disasters. These methods and practices are as below:

1. **Primary Methods of Social Work**

   The primary methods in social work practice include

   (a) Case Work

   (b) Group Work

   (c) Community Organization

2. **Secondary Methods of Social Work:**

   The secondary methods include

   (a) Social Welfare Administration

   (b) Social Work research

   (c) Social Action

   Let us now look at each one of the above-mentioned methods in social work in the context of disaster prevention, control and management.

Primary Methods in Social Work

(a) Casework

Casework is the earliest and probably the most widely discussed method of social work, pioneered originally by Octavia Hill in the London Charity Organisation Society. This method is taught in social work world over (Hamilton, 1951).

The significance of casework is its utility in handling individual cases and more specifically victims of disaster, accidents, trauma, and mental health issues and so on. This method will prove very useful in pre and post disaster situations. In the pre-disaster situations social workers who are experienced, trained and professional social workers can provide counseling to the individuals and families on preparedness, promotion of coping mechanism and mental health. They can create awareness among individuals and families about disaster management.

(b) Group Work

Yet another primary method in social work practice is group work. A group in a social work practice is seen as a self-managing unit. In simple terms, the group process leads to a spirit of cooperation, coordination and commonly understood procedures (Mujawar and Sardar, 2010).

Groups are particularly good at combining talents in providing innovative solutions to possible unfamiliar problems; in cases where there is no well-established approach/procedure, the wider skill and knowledge has a distinct advantage over that of the individual.

The range of scales provided by its members and the self-monitoring each group performs makes it a reasonably safe recipient for the delegated responsibility. Even if a problem could be decided by a single person, there are two main benefits and involving the people who carry out the decision. Firstly, the motivational aspect of participating in the decision will clearly enhance its implementation. Secondly, there may be factors which the implementer understands better than the single person who could supposedly have decided alone.

Group Development: It is common to view that development of a group as having four stages. These stages are:

Forming: Forming is the first stage when members come together, everybody is polite and dull initially, conflict is seldom voiced directly, mainly personal and definitely destructive. The group tends to defer to a large extent to those who emerge as leaders.

Storming: Storming is the next stage when all "hell" breaks loose and leaders are lynched, Factions form, personalities clash, no one concedes a single point. Storming contributes to make the picture of the group clear or even come into focus.

Norming: The third stage is norming, at this stage the subgroup begins to recognize the merits of working together and the infighting subsides. Since a new spirit of cooperation is evident, every member begins to feel secure in expressing their own view points and these are discussed openly with the whole group. However, at this stage methods become established and recognized by the group as a whole.

Performing: This is the culmination stage, when the group settles on the system, which allows free and frank exchange of views and high degree of support by the group for each other and its own decisions.

There are two main set of skills, which the group must require:

(a) Managerial Skills

(b) Interpersonal Skills

The combination of these skills contributes in accelerating the activities of the group.

(i) Accelerating development

It is common practice in accelerating group development to appoint and if necessary train a group facilitator. The role of this person is to continually draw the group attention to the group process and the goal to be achieved.

(ii) Mutual aid as group work technology

Mutual aid as group work technology can be understood as an exchange of help wherein the group member is both provider as well as the recipient of help in service of achieving common, group and individual goals. The rationales for cultivating mutual aid in the group encounter on mutual aid's resonance with humanistic values.

(a) Members have strengths, opinions, perspectives, information and experiences that can be drawn upon to help others in the group.

(b) Helping others helps the helper.

(c) Some type of help such as confrontation, are better received when emanating from peer, rather than the workers.

Group work thus, becomes very significant when it comes to disaster management situations. The management team needs to take a note of the about discussion on group work in professional practice.

(c) Community Organization

In a diverse culture, religious, linguistic and ethnic background of the target groups in India, it becomes difficult to organize a community, especially in a chaos situation, when a natural or man-made disasters occurs. Organizing the community is one of the difficult tasks. Robin and Peters (1990); Robin and Kharche (2015) have emphasized the need of rapport building and community organization.

The professional social workers or the members of disaster management team need to build confidence among people, listen to them, be patient with them and develop a close rapport with them. Once people accept them, they accept your views, ideas and start cooperating with them and this is the beginning of community organization. The primary method in social work becomes very handy in disaster management.

(i) Secondary Methods in Social Work Practice

Given the above background, it is important towards understanding the significance of secondary methods in social work practice.

(a) **Social Work Research:** Research is an ongoing and continuous process. Professional social workers value research and its significance in disaster management. Some of the areas of research that social workers probe into are:

- Vulnerable geographical zones and areas of disasters
- Causes of natural and man-made disasters
- Nature and role of disaster management agencies
- Quality of relief and rehabilitation services
- Psychosocial impact of disasters on survivors
- Policy issues with respect to compensation of property, damages and lives
- Administrative and political hurdles in disaster management
- Displacement issues in disaster affected area
- Risk factors related to disaster
- Counseling and mental health needs and so on
- Disaster-related stresses (fear of death or serious injury, prolonged displacement, separation from family.

(b) **Social Welfare Administration**

Social Welfare Administration is the practice of proficiently providing resources and services to meet the needs of the individuals, families, groups and communities to assist social relationship and adjustment needed for social functioning and prevention of social dysfunctions. What is planned must be implemented; what is implemented must be monitored; what is monitored must be followed up and evaluated, so as to know its success or failure. Social welfare Administration in this context becomes very significant as the professional social workers, who have the skill to administer and execute welfare activities, must apply this method so as to properly manage situations of various disasters that occurs world over. The secondary method of Social Welfare Administration hence becomes very handy in disaster management.

(c) **Social Action**

The concept of social action isn't it differently in sociology and social work. In sociology, it revolves around theoretical discussions whereas in social work, it is more practical. In social work, the term social action points out actually getting down to practical work in the field or at grassroots level (Hathaway N, 1914-40).

A professional social workers who has both theoretical and practical knowledge of social action, makes use of it, while handling disaster management issues. Thus, this secondary tool also contributes disaster management (Brown EL 1942, Dillick S., 1953, Burtym Z 1976).

Significance of Social Work Interventions

Social work as a profession have substantially contributed to the study results on environmental disasters, disaster related trauma, traumatic stress, psychosocial impact on affected community, disaster volunteers, at risk populations, organizations and networks, cross-cultural issues in disasters, research methods, measurement and theory. Social workers in disaster research have principally drawn knowledge-base from the multidisciplinary fields such as sociology, psychology, public health, anthropology, economics and political science.

Professional social workers and development experts engaged and associated with disaster management develop need-based interventions that are eco-culturally appropriate and acceptable to the local community. Post disaster situations demand eco-culture friendly interventions, for example, Malin village that was swallowed by a massive landslide was predominantly inhabited by tribe people called Koli Mahadev. The main occupation of this tribe was rice cultivation and they had a culture specific design of their traditional houses. In such a situation, the development planners ought to know the People's (insider's view) perception about their traditional house design, the construction rituals and ceremonies, and accordingly plan eco-culturally acceptable models of houses as per community needs and rehabilitate the survivors those who lost their houses in the disaster. However, given here is just one example, but social work practice can offer a greater deal of expertise, services and consultancy in the prevention, control and management of natural and man-made disasters. Some of the gaps in social work knowledge, and suggestions for future research may require further systematic investigation. Therefore, finally we may derive at the evidenced based substantive recommendations and suggestions for emergency management and social work interventions which may be relevant at a local, national and international level.

References

Adams R, (1999) Earthquake, Natural Disaster Management, Tudor Rose Holding Ltd. 52-54.

Andharia Janki (2013) Vulnerability and Disaster: Conceptual Contours of a People-centered View, In Parasuraman and Krishnan (eds.), India Disasters Report ii, Oxford University Press, New Delhi.

Babhulkar Rashmi, (2014). Psychological Rehabilitation of Earthquake Victims in Killari Village: An Experience.

Bankoff G., (2001). Rendering the World Unsafe: Vulnerability as Western Discourse, Disasters 25 (1) 19-35.

Biswas Nilanjana (2014) Gender and Disaster. In India Disasters Report II: Redefining Disasters, Edited by S. Parasuraman and Unni Krishnan, Oxford University Press.

Biswas Partha, (2014) 150 Missing, Rain Hampers Rescue Operation, Land Slide Swallows Pune Village, in The Indian Express, Date 31st July, 2014, Pune Edition.

Brown E.L, (1942) Social Work as a Profession, Russel Sage Foundation, New York.

Chandra. P. (2011). Disaster Preparedness and Rehabilitation. Arise Publishers and Distributors, New Delhi.

Choudhary R.S. (2014). Disaster Management Policy in India, in K.S. Patil and Others (eds.), Disaster Management in Higher Education, BSPK Publisher, Nagpur.

Indian Express (2014). Malin: District Administration takes Stock of Property Damage, The Indian Express, Nambiar Nisha, August 10th, 2014. At indianexpress.com

Indian Express (2014). "Malin, Day 6: Body Count Reaches 134". 5 August 2014.

International Federation of Red Cross and Red Crescent Societies (2017). "What is a Disaster?". www.ifrc.org. Retrieved 21 June 2017.

Jaswal S. and J. Joseph, (2013). Vidarbha Baseline Survey of Psychosocial Well-being. TISS Working Paper No. 4 April 2013. Available at http://rnd.tiss.edu/wp-content/uploads/2015/03/4-Surinder-Jaswal-and-other.pdf

Joshi Prasad, (2014). Children in Malin Clueless about P.M. Speech in Pune News Line Dated, September 6th, 2014, Pune.

Kadam Shivaji and Others (eds), (2010) Perspectives on Governance of Higher Education, Bharati Vidyapeeth, Pune.

Kasturi Pesala, (2014). Role of IGNOU in Andaman and Nicobar Islands, in Patil K.S. and Tribhuvan Robin (eds.), Social Problems and Development Issues of Youth, Discovery Publishing House, New Delhi.

Kreps, G. (1984). Sociological Inquiries and Disaster Research, Annual Review of Sociology, Vol. 10 pp. 309-30.

Kulkarni, S., (2014) Land Slide: 300 NDRF Personnel Race with Time on Rough Terrain, in Pune News Line, Dated July 31st, 2014, Pune Edition.

Kulkarni, Sushant, (2014). More Bodies Found, Toll up to in Pune Newsline, Dated 1st August, 2014, Pune Edition.

Mahapatra Richard (2013) Drought: Threatening Food Security.

Marathe P.P. (2006) Concepts and Practices in Disaster Management, Diamond Publication, Pune.

Merriam-Webster (2018). "Disaster." Merriam-Webster.com, Merriam-Webster, www.merriam-webster.com/dictionary/disaster. Accessed 28 May 2018.

Mujawar W.R and Sardar N.K. (2010). Field Work Training in Social Work, Maugalam Publication, New Delhi.

NIDM (2014). National Institute of Disaster Management, Ministry of Home Affairs, GOI, at http://www.nidm.gov.in 2014.

Oliver-Smith A (2010). World Disasters Report, 2010 IFRC

Online Epistemology Dictionary (2018) at https://www.etymonline.com/word/disaster.

Oxford (2010). Oxford Dictionary of English, 3rd Edition, Oxford. ISBN : 9780199571123, 0199571120.

Parasuraman S., Krishnan Unni, (2013). India Disaster Report II: Redefining Disasters, Oxford University Press, New Delhi.

Patil, K.S. and others (eds), (2014) Disaster Management in Higher Education, BSPK Publisher, Nagpur.

Patil, Pranali K., (2014) A Study of Disaster Management in Kedarnath Patil, K.S. and Others (eds), (2014) Disaster Management in Higher Education, BSPK Publisher, Nagpur.

Paul B.K, (2011). Environmental Hazards and Disasters, Wiley-Blackwell, New Delhi.

Pradhan Narendra, (2009) Disaster Management, Surendra Publication, New Delhi.

Quarantelli, E. and R. Dynes (1970). Property Norms and Looting: Their Patterns in Community Crisis, Phylon Vol. 31 No. 2 pp. 168-82.

Raphael, B. & Middleton, W. (1987). Mental Health Responses in a Decade of Disasters: Australia, 1874-1983. Hospital and Community Psychiatry, 38, 1331-1337.

Rathod Sudhir, (2014) Report on Uttarakhand Disaster Management, (With Reference to Kedarnath Valley) Including Lessons Learnt, Centre for Disaster Management, YASHADA, Pune.

Sakal (2014). Lakh Rupees for Malin Village, on Dated 6th September (2014), Pune.

Sangameshwar and Kulkarni A.V, (2011) Observational Studies of Recent Past- Chp 3, A Report of the Study of Himalayan Glaciers, PSA/2011/12.

Sangameshwar and Shukla S.P., (2009). Inventory of Himalayan Glaciers: A Contribution to the International Hydrological Programme (Special Publication No. 34, Geological Survey of India): An Updated Edition. GSI, 2009, Reprint.

Sharma Arjun K, (2012). Natural and Manmade Disasters, Akhand Publishing House, New Delhi.

Shripad D., (2013). Dipping Water Levels: Looming Crisis. In Parasuraman and Krishnan (eds.), India Disasters Report ii, Oxford University Press, New Delhi.

Singh K.K and Others, (eds), (2010). Manmade Disasters, A.P. TT, Publishing Corporation, New Delhi.

Singh Sarthak, (2010). Disaster Management, Oxford University Press, New Delhi.

Singh, R.B. (2006). Natural Hazards and Disaster Management, Rawat Publications, New Delhi.

Suri S., (2000). Orissa Disaster: Agony of the Living, Authors Press, New Delhi.

Talwar, A.K. and Juneja Satish, (2009) Tsunami Disaster Management, Commonwealth Publishers, New Delhi, 28-49.

Taori K. (2005). Disaster Management through Panchayat Raj, Concept Publishing House.

Thakkar H. (2013). The Strange Case of India's Missing Dams. The News in Proportion. IndiTogether. 08 March 2013. Available at: http://indiatogether.org/dams-environment.

Thakur, A.K. and Patil, G.V.K, (2012) Disaster Management and Climate Change, Regal Publications, New Delhi.

Turner Berry, A. and Nick, F. Pidgeon, (1977). Manmade Disasters. Butterworth Heinjeman: Oxford, UN Dept of Humanitarian Affairs.

UNDP (2018). Sustainable Development Goals, Available at http://www.UNDP.org/content/undp/en/home.html

UN-ISDR, (2004). Living with Risk: A Global Review of Disaster Reduction Initiatives, Geneva.

UNISDR, 2018. United Nations Office for Disaster Risk Reduction (2018), at https://www.unisdr.org/we/inform/terminology

United Nations, (2018) Note that the Resident Coordinator Reports to the Emergency Relief Coordinator. Accessed on 10 June 2018 at http://legal.un.org/ilc/sessions/61/pdfs/english/pop_ocha.pdf

WHO (2002). "Disasters and Emergencies Definitions". Training Package WHO/EHA Panafrican Emergency Training Centre, Addis Ababa: Emergency Humanitarian Action. March 2002.

World Bank, (2018). Disaster Risk Management: Overview available at http://www.worldbank.org/en/topic/disasterriskmanagement/overview

Index

E

F

G